Leo P. Hennigan, M.D.

A CONSPIRACY of SILENCE: ALCOHOLISM

Gannel Publications
Bethesda, Maryland

A CONSPIRACY of SILENCE: ALCOHOLISM

published by: Gannel Publications
P.O. Box 30836
Bethesda, Maryland 20824
printed in the United States of America

Library of Congress Cataloging in Publication Data
Hennigan: Dr. Leo P.
A CONSPIRACY OF SILENCE: ALCOHOLISM
by Leo P. Hennigan, M.D.

ISBN 0-9626 382-2-6 $17.95 softcover
LCC 90-81380
cover art and illustrations by Joe Sutliff, Veda Design Group
typography by John Marshall, Veda Design Group
co editors: Anne Bradford and Shirley Onie
printing and binding by Haddon Craftsmen, Inc., Scranton Pa.

To Mary McGinn Taylor
without whose belief in me
this book would not have been written.

• • •

The two who helped me the most
during my trying years —
the kindest person I ever knew,
my brother-in-law
Roland Tanck, Ph.D.
and my sister Helen Tanck

• • •

To the alcoholics in AA
who saved my life.

TABLE OF CONTENTS

ACKNOWLEDGMENTS

The writing and publication of this book has been a long and difficult, but rewarding experience. I would not have ever considered embarking on this journey were it not for the encouragement of Mary Taylor who originally suggested I write it.

I remember and wish to thank Peter Sterrantino, whose confrontation led to my recovery and saved my life; and Dr. Frank Cresswell, Jr. the one doctor in 27 years who recognized my pain and set me free.

Once I had gathered my thoughts, it was Noreen O'Meara Shambacher who helped me to organize them properly and Catherine Foreman who, with great care, processed and reprocessed my manuscript.

Anne Bradford, co-editor, spent many hours on this project. The cover artwork was created by Joe Sutliff, who was so successful in visually interpreting my deep feeling. John Marshall designed and produced the typography.

My gratitude to the medical schools in the United States and Canada who responded to my survey with an open mind, and Maxwell Weisman, M.D. whose review of my manuscript led to thoughtful and appropriate changes.

My special thanks to Sonia Arisch, whose support and encouragement made this difficult task easier. And finally to Shirley Onie, co-editor, who was involved in every aspect and offered her intellect, good judgment, creativity and friendship, thank you.

Last but certainly not least, I want to thank Anthony Kniolek of Haddon Craftsmen, Inc. of Scranton, Pennsylvania, for bringing my manuscript into print. His kindness, patience and many suggestions are very much appreciated.

PREFACE

No matter who you are, your life has been touched by a mysterious, widespread disease. The disease is often unrecognized. It is often undiagnosed. More often, it is denied. Yet it is eating into the very fabric of our society. Although you may not have this disease, you are aware of others suffering from it -- a spouse, a parent, a child, an uncle or aunt, a friend, a co-worker. Everyday we read of people killed by this disease -- either as heart or liver give way -- or by accidents. Yet very little is said or done to treat this disease. It is cloaked in what I choose to call "A Conspiracy of Silence." The disease is alcoholism.

This book will tell you, by personal story and medical facts, exactly what alcoholism is. This book will explain that alcoholism is, in fact, a simple disease -- one that can be easily diagnosed and easily treated.

The first part of the book is my story, the story of an alcoholic who finally recovered after some 27 years of misguided treatment. With variations, my story is every alcoholic's story. You will probably wonder -- as my editors did -- how could such a sick person recover.

The second part of the book presents some new, some better-known and some controversial diagnostic methods for dealing with this disease. You may be surprised, disagree or question the validity of some simple techniques used to detect alcoholism. For example, can you stop right now and remember all the details about your first drink? Do you know what is meant by "positive confrontation?" Do you have preconceived notions about the people who might attend a meeting of Alcoholics Anonymous (AA)?

In another chapter of Part II, we discuss what training -- if any -- doctors and therapists are given for treating alcoholism. You may be surprised at what a survey of medical schools revealed.

Finally, after we discuss the families of alcoholics, attitudes held by the general public, and the medical community, we present an all out appeal to you and to members of AA.

If we -- you and I -- focus on the suggestions of Part II, we could become part of a movement that could conquer this disease -- that could end this conspiracy of silence. To end the conspiracy is to begin creating a healthier society. We could save lives. And, as the Talmud says, *"If you save one life, it is as if you saved the world."*

INTRODUCTION

Alcoholism is a disease characterized by denial. The denial is seen in the medical profession where there is an unwritten law: Thou shalt not diagnose alcoholism until it is in its advanced stages. Alcoholism is denied by physicians, psychologists, social workers, and nurses, all of whom feel it is quite acceptable not to ask questions about alcohol. Parents deny it when told that one of their children is an alcoholic; husbands and wives deny it when told their spouse is an alcoholic; friends deny it when they look the other way and ignore the drinking habits of their associates. I think of alcoholism as the "ostrich syndrome." Most Americans have their heads in the sand when faced with the problem of alcoholism. An interesting aspect, also, is that the deniers have no trouble in pointing their collective fingers at the victim, the alcoholic, and accusing him of being guilty of what they are guilty of -- denial.

Despite the numerous books and articles that have been written about our number one health problem, most Americans are still confused about what alcoholism is -- and what to do about it. I use the term number one health problem since alcoholism contributes to heart disease, strokes, accidents, and a myriad of other illnesses.

Alcoholism is confusing and mysterious because we have made it so. I intend to take away the confusion and mystery concerning alcoholism and reduce it to some very simple facts that can be understood by all.

I am a recovered alcoholic. I am also a psychiatrist. Either way, I am amazed at how ineptly my alcoholism was dealt with by members of my profession -- both by those treating me as a patient and by those who were co-workers or friends.

I am equally amazed at how others in my life were just as unable to help me, not because they didn't care, but because they lacked essential information-- information which I will present and discuss in this book. Very little has been done to determine why alcoholism remains our number one health problem. I have looked into this carefully, and I have some very simple answers to this dilemma.

Written with the basic philosophy of Alcoholics Anonymous, "Keep It Simple," this book will avoid medical or scientific jargon. I shall write more like an alcoholic who is a psychiatrist, than like a psychiatrist who is an alcoholic.

Some popular beliefs about alcoholism are:

1. The alcoholic can't be helped unless he admits he is an alcoholic.

2. The alcoholic can't be helped unless he or she wants to stop drinking.

3. Alcoholism is a very complicated disease, difficult to diagnose and difficult to treat.

All of the above statements are false. However, since our society wants them to be true, society believes them to be true and puts the responsibility for getting well on the one who can do the least about starting treatment -- the patient, the alcoholic.

I would like you to join me on a journey through my alcoholism: starting with my first drink, going step by step with me through all the symptoms, my eventual recovery, my annoyance at how badly alcoholism is dealt with, and finally my question to myself, "What are you going to do about it?" Thus, my decision to write this book.

For this book to have any validity, I must speak quite frankly about the poor treatment I received at the hands of a number of my fellow physicians. I want to make it clear that most of them were conscientious, sincere, and wellmeaning. They intended nothing but good, but were hampered by the ignorance and attitudes of the time. Regrettably, much of the same ignorance and the same attitudes are still with us today.

To help you understand alcoholism, I have listed at the end of this introduction each symptom or stage. During the telling of my story, the symptoms are in bold face.

Since alcoholism has an effect on every aspect of the victim's life, it is necessary for me to mention the various emotional problems I had before I began drinking, also during the drinking phase of my alcoholism, and then what happened during my recovery.

Although my problems were severe and became aggravated by my alcoholism, I want to make it clear that my problems did not cause my alcoholism. I may have been genetically predisposed to become an alcoholic once I began drinking. Even had I been an emotional "Rock of Gibraltar," my drinking probably would have resulted in alcoholism.

As the reader of yet another book on alcoholism, you have a right to know what to expect. These are my promises to you:

1. You will find everything I say to be uncomplicated and easy to understand.

2. You will see alcoholism presented from a totally different perspective.

3. You will be offered answers, not questions.

4. You will learn that alcoholism is not a complicated disease, but a simple one which we have complicated by our approach to it.

5. You will learn how you, regardless of your educational background, can become a member of a large team with one goal:

Changing alcoholism from our number one health problem to a very simple, easily diagnosed, and easily treated illness.

Before we begin, I have one request to make of you, a request that will greatly enhance your understanding of alcoholism and the alcoholic. Put aside all your opinions, beliefs, attitudes, and convictions about alcoholism and the alcoholic. I promise you it will pay dividends.

Try to imagine, as we begin this journey, that we are in a comfortable living room. We have been talking about various subjects, and when the subject of alcoholism comes up, you ask me to tell you about my alcoholism and my recovery from it.

SYMPTOMS OF ALCOHOLISM

These symptoms are listed in the order in which they occurred in my progressive alcoholism. However, the order of occurrence may vary.

- Occasional relief drinking -- first symptom of alcoholism.
- Increase in alcohol tolerance.
- Controlled drinking.
- Increased dependency on alcohol.
- Avoiding friends and family.
- Rationalizing one's drinking.
- Surreptitious drinking.
- Efforts to control drinking fail more often.
- Inability to limit consumption.
- Geographic cure -- moving in the hope one's drinking will lessen.
- Urgency of first drink.
- Onset of blackouts.
- Unpredictability of the alcoholic's drinking.
- Promises to self and others fail.
- Annoyance when people talk about our drinking.
- Loss of other interests.
- Neglect of food.
- Onset of tremors.
- Early morning drink.
- Undefinable fears.
- Impaired thinking.
- Hopelessness.
- Telephonitis.
- Missing work on Mondays.
- Decrease in alcohol tolerance.
- Drinking for oblivion.
- Complete defeat -- surrender (a willingness to face one's drinking).
- Increased feeling of hope -- first sign of recovery.

A CONSPIRACY of SILENCE: ALCOHOLISM

"An honest tale speeds best
being plainly told."
— Richard III, Shakespeare

PART ONE

My Story

1. EARLY YEARS

"Oh, I have passed a miserable night, so full of ugly sights, of ghostly dreams, that, as I am a Christian faithful man, I would not spend another such night, though 'twere to buy a world of happy days."

— Richard III, Shakespeare

It was 4 a.m. I was living in my city apartment, I found myself wide awake. I heard a loud noise. It was as if a plane were flying down the nearby street. I heard another sound -- another plane -- and then another and another. There was only one logical explanation - they were Russian airplanes!

When I finally summoned up my courage, I crawled to the front window. I looked out. I saw only trucks going down the street. I was still shaking from the fear that gripped me.

This fear -- this terror -- is an emotion that often engulfs an alcoholic. That's what I was then -- but didn't seem to know it at the time. This fear distorted my perception of reality and impaired my thinking.

Although different from early childhood fear, I would, at these times, be reminded of my fear of death. This fear developed when, as a young child, I would be held up to kiss a dead relative. When my baby brother died, I was only five. About then, a relative, looking me sternly in the eye, said "Someday you too will die." Such a practice stemmed from Irish wakes -- much in vogue in the 1920s among Irish Catholics living in Old Forge, Pennsylvania. Here was where my father worked, initially as a coal miner. Shortly after I was born on October 2, 1921, to Patrick Lawrence Hennigan and Genevieve Kearns Hennigan, my father changed his occupation to become an agent of an insurance company.

When I was age 12, my father had me taste some port wine. The tiny sip tasted so horrible, I didn't taste any alcohol again for 12 years.

My growing up years included walking in nearby woods and learning to love the beauty of nature. Although I had six older siblings and one younger, I was given violin lessons and later piano. Through my brothers and sisters, I developed a love of good literature -- the writings of Thomas Wolfe, Willa Cather, Sigrid Undset, Maupassant, Boccaccio and Shakespeare.

Sports -- except for pool and bowling -- were out because of my small size. I enjoyed participating in the school orchestra. One time the orchestra director, Peter Samoney, asked Wally Fitzsimmons and me to remain after rehearsal. My immediate reaction was "What did I do wrong?" This was my typical response as my family seldom gave compliments. I had little self esteem -- a condition that pervaded my life for many years.

In high school I was an indifferent student. I wanted a low profile and settled for finishing in the middle of a class of 169. At that time, St. Thomas College, now the University of Scranton, gave exams to any male (it was a men's college) in Lackawanna County, and on the basis of high scores awarded 10 scholarships. Among the many who took the test, I was the only one from my school who was not an honor student. I came in 13th in the county and highest in my high school. The next highest placed 30th. When I heard how well I had done, my first thought was that there was a mistake, my papers were mixed up in error.

Another such episode occurred in 1979 when my bridge partner, Marie Trossevin and I played in a yearly charity game sponsored by the American Contract Bridge League. In this continent-wide contest, we came in first in the novice class. When I heard this, my first thought was there was probably a computer error.

While in high school, I was unsure of my future career. I thought of music, but realized that my enthusiasm was much greater than my ability. I considered law since Clarence Darrow was one of my childhood heroes, but ruled this out because of my fear of public speaking; to me a lawyer had to appear in court.

On graduating from high school in 1939, I took a summer job as a busboy at the Lido Hotel on Long Island, and then, for the rest of the summer, as a waiter on the boardwalk. This was my first work experience and my first time away from home. Of four of us from Scranton, two were students at St. Thomas College and two were to become students there in September. One became a priest, two became obstetricians, and I became a psychiatrist.

St. Thomas College was run by the Christian Brothers until my senior year when it became a Jesuit college and was renamed the University of Scranton. I entered St. Thomas in September 1939 as a premedical student. Two years later America entered the war; and in January 1943, I graduated from the University.

Having been accepted into Georgetown Medical School, I had to choose between that and the military. I did alot of soul-searching about whether I was qualified to be a doctor. Would I be able to concentrate on studies? How would I feel later on if I had not been in the war? I finally decided to enter the military, hoping to do something heroic.

WAR EXPERIENCES

The various services were recruiting college graduates for Officers' Candidate School. Since those who became officers by this route were referred to as "90-day wonders", and my self-doubts came to the fore, I did not choose to ask for a commission. I joined the Army, and on April 10, 1943, left Scranton and was sent to Camp Grant in Rockford, Illinois, for basic training in the medical corps.

It has been said that being in a war is often one of the most meaningful, exciting experiences that many men have. Yes, I felt pleased to think that I was doing something noble. It was a popular war for a popular cause. Germany had conquered many countries, the Japanese had bombed Pearl Harbor, and both had to be defeated.

My months in basic training were neither particularly good nor bad. I was pleased that as a non-athlete who had had a relatively easy life, I kept up with the others on all hikes, obstacle courses, and other facets of basic training. Whenever I am in a new situation or a new location, I always try to see it as a new adventure, and that is how I viewed being in the service. I had never been more than 200 miles from home, and the idea of travel excited me even though I also had the normal fear of combat.

While in basic training, I was one of several in my company interviewed for Officers' Candidate School in medical administration. I said I preferred the artillery or the infantry, but it didn't make any difference what I preferred and it was the last I heard of it. This may have been very fortunate, because the death rate for junior officers was extremely high.

After basic training we went to Camp San Luis Obispo in California for more training while waiting to go to the southwest Pacific. From there we went to Camp Stoneman and then on to Hawaii.

While still within sight of San Quentin, I experienced one of my most unpleasant memories of World War II -- sea sickness. We eventually arrived in Honolulu, and the next few months were spent in jungle warfare training at Scofield Barracks. I was to return to Hawaii twelve years later, but I am getting ahead of my story.

Until I was in Hawaii I had never held a rifle. It had been learned that the Japanese were disregarding the Geneva Convention so medics learned to use a rifle and were armed from then on. I was coming closer to combat.

Sometime in late November or early December of 1943, my outfit boarded a luxury liner, converted to a troopship, for a two-week trip to New Guinea. We arrived at Milne Bay, New Guinea, sometime in December and began combat training.

New Guinea was solid jungle, it rained daily and life there was not like being at The Hilton. I was in Company D of the Sixth Medical Battalion of the Sixth Infantry Division. Companies A, B, and C collected the injured from the battlefields. My outfit was a clearing station to which Companies A, B, and C took the injured.

Sometime in 1944 we landed at New Guinea's Maffin Bay Beach -- still facing solid jungle. For the rest of that day, we cut down trees and set up tents. That evening, Lou, a former neighbor who was my age and inducted into the army the same day I was, came to our clearing station as one of our first casualties. En route to guard duty, I told Lou I would see him the next day. When I went to see him the next morning, I found he had died during the night. He lived on the street next to me, and I had known him since childhood. He was the first casualty I experienced during the war.

Our division saw much combat and had many casualties. To have the ocean on one side and the jungle and the enemy on the other is not the most pleasant of experiences. Many nights I wondered if I would ever see another sunrise.

After a few months on Maffin Bay, we moved to Sansapor, New Guinea. There we had even more combat. We were now preparing for the invasion of Luzon, the largest Island in the Philippines. The war was now in our favor. On the evening of January 3, 1945, while getting ready for our landing the next day, I heard Tokyo Rose on the radio. She mentioned our division by number and that we were going to land at Lingayan Gulf and said they had a nice party ready for us.

We landed at Lingayan Gulf on January 4, 1945. I saw General Douglas MacArthur and his entourage walking up the beach. We landed unopposed but later faced a great deal of combat.

We were still on Luzon when Clarence Swanson from Minnesota rushed into our tent and told us about the atomic bomb being dropped on Hiroshima. When he described how powerful it was, we didn't believe him, mainly because Clarence was known to embellish stories a bit, but this time he was right. We welcomed this and the bombing of Nagasaki because we were anticipating landing on mainland Japan, with the possibility of a million casualties.

For me on Luzon, there was one pleasant break. My youngest

brother, Paul, sergeant in the Air Force, flew from Leyte to Manila to visit me. He was trying to hitch a ride outside of Manila when Sergeant Bratcher from my outfit saw him. Noting a family resemblance, Sergeant Bratcher stopped and asked if he were looking for Leo. Thus, Paul and I had a few pleasant days together.

The night the war ended, I was with my outfit in northern Luzon. The men decided I should finally have a beer. When we received beer, I had always traded it for CocaCola. This time, they urged me until I drank a can of beer and became very sick. I later found out it was mostly medical alcohol.

Those who were married and had children were the first to be discharged; the rest of my outfit were sent to Korea. After a stormy voyage, we finally landed in late 1945. I had been used to the tropics for the better part of two years, so Korea seemed very cold. As we were marching to the train after we landed, I heard a brokendown Victrola playing "Lady of Spain," and saw a sign over the railroad tracks saying, "Welcome apostles of justice, hear our cries of joy, long have we awaited your arrival."

For the next few months I waited to leave for home and started to eat better. I had survived the war. Now I had to face sea sickness -- not just sea sickness itself but being cramped in a troopship for days and days with its limited sanitary facilities and its odors. Time passed, however, and the unpleasantness was offset by the knowledge that after 33 months away, with no furlough, I was going home.

How can I describe my feelings as we approached Tacoma, Washington, on December 17, 1945, and saw the lights and the shore appear? There was, of course, gratitude that I made it, and gratitude that all three of my brothers made it. There was relief, too, relief that it was finally over, the battles left behind. Little did I realize that within a few weeks, I would begin a personal battle that would last 27 years and would make my military duty pale by comparison.

The next few weeks were occupied with the usual paperwork of processing out of the service. I had hoped to be home for Christmas but this was not to be. I finally arrived at Indiantown Gap, Pennsylvania, and was discharged on a Friday in January 1946. From there I traveled by bus to Wilkes-Barre and then on to Old Forge, twelve miles away.

POSTWAR YEARS

My sister Loretta was home when I arrived in the evening and after spending some time with her, I went to meet my father who was with several of his friends. It was a very beautiful reunion, and I think we both felt very close to each other then.

My older brother Al had already been discharged from the Air Force. Paul returned from Leyte the following Friday, and the Friday after that, John, a physician with the Eighth Air Force in England, returned home. All four of us had come home uninjured, three of us having been in combat.

This was a wonderful time in my life. Except for recent years, it was the happiest time. All four brothers were together, I had the use of a car, and was receiving $20 a week from the government. My younger brother, Paul, and I were now good friends, and thanks to his being more socially aggressive than I, my social life was better than ever.

After I had met with all my family, I visited Mrs. Renna, mother of my friend Joe, to find out when he was due to return. Since her information was vague, I called Joe's girlfriend, Helen, to see if she had any more information. She and I went to a restaurant now called Sea Seas in Moosic. That was where I had what I think of as my first drink. One glass of wine with SevenUp. I had only one drink that night, but it was the beginning of my drinking. From that time on, alcohol became an important part of my life.

Why did I decide to begin drinking at the age of 24? There were two reasons: I neither drank nor smoked before the war and was often kidded about this. I thought if I ordered an alcoholic beverage, there would be less kidding. Second, and I believe more important, was that I had by now begun to associate drinking with being a man, being an adult, being sophisticated. Since I felt I was not any of these, it was time to begin drinking. To me, drinking was something adults did. At that time I had not the slightest idea what effect alcohol had, and certainly had not the least concept of what alcoholism was.

The bold type in the next chapters are the symptoms of alcoholism as they occurred for me. I relate them as part of my story.

2. FIRST STAGES OF DRINKING

"Since the creation of the world there has been no tyrant like Intempertance, and no slaves so cruelly treated as his."

— William Lioyd Garrison

Occasional Relief Drinking -- First Symptom of Alcoholism. Although I don't remember any specific effect my first drink in January 1946 had, I do know that within the next few months I had learned that the effect of a few drinks was very pleasant. I enjoyed dating partly because of the drinking involved. A few drinks would make me feel more confident in social situations; I was more spontaneous, danced better (or thought I did), and my shyness diminished. In fact, I wondered why it took me so long to find this magic fluid, this nectar of the gods. During that time, I felt my life changing for the better, as I seemed to have gained some confidence as a result of my Army experiences. I began to look forward to a few drinks. I noted that I often had a drink or two more than my friends, but to me this meant I was keeping to the good old American tradition of a man being able to hold his liquor.

Increase in Alcohol Tolerance. I began to drink a little more each time, yet I felt that the drinks did not affect me as much. So I had to drink more for the desired effect.

Controlled Drinking. Nonalcoholics don't have to worry about drinking too much; they just don't. Sometime during the period from my first drink in January 1946 until September 1946, when I came to Washington, D.C., to begin my studies at Georgetown University Medical School, I had clearly fallen in love with alcohol. During this time, I seemed to have made a decision to have no more than four drinks which indicates that I was beginning to be concerned about my fondness for alcohol; and, in fact, that I wanted more to drink. I was beginning to see the necessity for controlling my drinking. I was now in early alcoholism.

My first year in medical school was a very difficult time. I had been away from studying for over three years, I had not developed good study habits, had little confidence to begin with, and, of course, had the usual severe pressures that go with being a freshman. I experienced a great deal of anxiety at that time, a condition which was to stay with me for many years.

Several months into the first year, my father had a heart attack. This necessitated my being home for some time. Missing so much school and the stress of my father's illness would have been fatal to my medical school career and I would have failed the first year had it not been for the help I received from a classmate and very dear friend, Dr. Ray Hayes, a psychiatrist who now lives in Louisville, Kentucky. While I was gone, he made carbon copies of all lectures and went over them with me upon my return. My father made an uneventful recovery and died nine years later.

The four years in medical school were not markedly significant as far as alcohol was concerned. I looked forward to the glow from a few drinks, but I was not as yet involved in solitary drinking.

When I graduated from medical school in June 1950, I accepted a two-year internship at St. Elizabeth's Hospital in Washington, D.C. I chose this hospital since it was a psychiatric hospital with 7,500 patients, and I had by now decided I was going to be a psychiatrist.

Increased Dependency on Alcohol. It was during my internship, I became more dependent on alcohol. I began to deal with anxiety, depression, and insomnia by drinking and withdrawing from others.

Avoiding Friends and Family. When people called, I said I was "too busy." Thus, I began to withdraw from family and friends and began thinking more about drinking.

Rationalizing One's Drinking. I rationalized drinking by saying to myself, "There's nothing wrong with drinking if you don't get drunk." Nonalcoholics don't need to do this.

Surreptitious Drinking. During my internship, my drinking became more secretive, and I started to hide my bottle of wine in such places as my piano.

Efforts to Control Fail More Often. I looked forward to parties to justify my heavy drinking, and began to experience situations in which my promises to myself to limit my drinks were beginning to fail.

Inability to Limit Consumption. When others were ready to stop, I was often the one to have just one more.

Despite my increasing dependence on alcohol and some gradual worsening of my previously mentioned symptoms, I now look back upon my two years at St. Elizabeth's as essentially quite happy. I felt the most difficult career preparation was over.

One episode I remember quite well had to do with a young priest who was there for a few months as part of his program in pastoral counseling. Someone said, "He seems to be drinking a bit too much," practically always a euphemism for alcoholism. Since I was a Catholic, it was suggested that I might keep an eye on him.

We were at a party when the hostess informed me that Father J. had too much to drink and asked me to drive him back to St. Elizabeth's. Because of his condition, I decided it was more than a one-man operation and enlisted the help of a fellow intern. He and I helped Father J., now quite drunk and boisterous, to his car, at which point I took over the driving. This was shocking because I had never seen a drunken priest before. We drove around trying to sober up Father J. Somewhere in suburbia, we had to stop because he had to urinate. We stopped at a partially-built housing development. Father J., upon getting out of the car, took off like a deer. Laughing and acting silly, he led us on a merry chase. He fell down a rain-washed, muddy hill. We had no choice but to follow him. Eventually we got him back in the car.

We spent hours driving around to sober up Father J., but without much success. During this time my companion added to my storehouse of Catholic knowledge by telling me that, according to tradition in the Catholic church, all the property of Franciscans (Father J. was a Franciscan) belongs to the Pope. At this point I said, "Bill, I never thought I would see the day when I would be driving a drunken priest around in the Pope's car." Our goal now was to sneak him into his room on the third floor of the center building at St. Elizabeth's. Considering he was still laughing and clowning and all three of us were covered with mud, it was like trying to sneak the sun past a rooster.

As I remember, we passed a few attendants who pretended to be blind and finally did get Father J. to his room. He was making so much noise we decided we had to sedate him. We enlisted the help of a fellow physician, who was a psychiatrist and friend of Father J. He began giving him a sedative intravenously. For a few seconds Father J. stopped breathing, but fortunately for only a few seconds.

I didn't know what to do about this incident. I was reluctant to report it to his superior. The next day, I discussed it with another young priest who was also there for pastoral counseling. He said he and Father J. were going to New York that week and he would discuss it with him. Fatherd J. never mentioned this episode, nor did I. Eventually our paths parted. We never thought of this as alcoholism.

Geographic Cure. Thinking that a change of geography would lessen my drinking, I ended my internship with thoughts of moving away. Eventually I accepted an offer from the Norwich State Hospital in Norwich, Connecticut.

I began my first year residency in psychiatry there on July 1, 1952. It was a very pleasant hospital in which to work. The staff was well trained, morale was excellent, and the overall working conditions fine. I have many fond memories of Norwich and the people there -- Dr. Ronald Kettle, the Superintendent, Dr. Conrad Ranger, the Assistant Superintendent, and two of the clinical directors.

I was given much responsibility. I accepted it willingly. I was well liked there and Dr. Kettle expressed a hope that upon finishing my training in psychiatry I would return. He indicated that I would be the type of person he would want in charge after he retired.

Because of my background, I was soon assigned to work with one doctor who was in charge of four buildings at the Norwich State Hospital. He had me take charge of two of the buildings. Another doctor who supervised three buildings said he hoped I could work for him. I soon decided I could finish my rounds on my two buildings and assist this doctor in his work, since he was involved in treating patients with electroshock therapy and insulin-coma therapy. I suggested this arrangement, and it was approved by all. I mention this situation to indicate the level of my functioning, my enthusiasm to learn, and my ability to organize things. This would change.

As always upon coming to a new place, I had driven about the area locating all the good restaurants and places of interest.

Urgency of First Drink. I soon began to note that I was beginning to look forward to the end of the work day so I could go to the local tavern and have a few beers. A colleague, Dr. Jerry Vogeler, mentioned in later years, that he had noted back in Norwich that I gulped rather than sipped my first drink. As time went on, I became more and more aware of how insecure I was and how I was using alcohol more and more to deal with anxiety, insomnia, and lack of confidence.

Onset of Blackouts. New Year's Eve of 1952 was very significant because a number of important firsts happened that night. There was to be a party at the home of a colleague. I was ill (unrelated to my drinking), so I planned on missing the party and going to bed early. About 8:00 p.m. I called in my regrets but was talked into coming over to have one drink. Since my stomach was upset, I didn't want my usual bourbon and water. Someone suggested I try something that had a better taste, a gin and tonic. I was going to have one drink and return home. However, I continued to drink until I passed out. The next thing I remember was coming to about 4:00 a.m., New Year's Day. Since this had never happened to me before, I couldn't appreciate its seriousness; thus, I felt I could drive home and did just that.

Since I was on duty the next morning, January 1, 1953, I arose early. When I got to my car I saw it was seriously damaged. I had no immediate recollection of what had happened. Later, I learned that I had been driving on the wrong side of the road and was involved in an accident. No charges were pressed because the other driver was a teenager driving without a license.

That night four things happened: I got drunk for the first time in my life; I had my first blackout; I had my first automobile accident under the influence of alcohol; for the first of many times, I swore I would never take another drink.

Unpredictability of the Alcoholic's Drinking. I really intended having only one drink. This is one of the most diagnostic signs of alcoholism: the person saying to himself or others, "Tonight I'm going to have (any number) . . . ," but he exceeds it. It needn't happen with each drinking episode. The feelings of guilt, remorse, embarrassment, and depression were very profound and no doubt I worked harder at "controlling" my drinking. But clearly my illness was progressing and my ability to "control" my drinking was slipping.

I emphasize controlling because if you have to work hard to control your drinking, it's a problem, and if it's a problem with drinking, it's alcoholism.

Promises to Self and Others Fail. The promise I made to myself on New Year's Eve to have only one drink failed. My other promises to myself failed as well. When I first arrived in Connecticut, weekends were first used for dating or for visiting places like Mystic, New York City, or Boston. As the year progressed, I began to see weekends as a time when I could be by myself in my apartment drinking.

With the academic year ending, I began thinking of where I would go for my second and third year of study. I wanted to leave after one year because I wanted a variety of experiences, but there is no doubt

I was continuing my attempt at a geographic cure. This is tied to the alcoholic's erroneous notion that he drinks because he has problems, when the truth is he has problems because he drinks.

Another Geographic Cure. When I left Connecticut in June 1953, I went to Ypsilanti State Hospital at Ypsilanti, Michigan. I was to remain there for my second and third year of training in psychiatry. As usual, upon coming to a new place, my drinking seemed to lessen. I was involved in availing myself of the cultural opportunities in Detroit and Ann Arbor and seeing various athletic activities at the University of Michigan. The staff at all levels worked well with each other and there was a minimum of interpersonal difficulties, largely because of the benevolent, gentle way of Dr. Yoder, the superintendent, which filtered down from him to the rest of us.

Let me recount one incident that demonstrated the hospital's philosophy. We had a daily meeting at 8:00 a.m., at which time the chief social worker would read letters from various patients' families who wanted to take the patient home for the weekend. The doctor in charge of the ward would then discuss the specific patient with the ward attendant. The ward attendant's recommendation would usually determine the doctor's approval or disapproval of the visit.

One day Dr. Yoder called me into his office regarding an 18-year-old for whom I approved a weekend pass. He very gently suggested that maybe I had overlooked a certain note of his that the patient, being a pyromaniac, was not a candidate for visits. He allowed me to change the order without making it seem as if I had committed a grave error.

Several weeks later, while making rounds, two attendants were having some difficulty with a patient who was obviously very disturbed. They stated the family was there for the patient since his going on a visit had been approved by Dr. Yoder. I called Dr. Yoder and indicated the potential danger of the patient jumping out of the car. He had the family and patient come to his office, at which time the order was rescinded. This was another example of the pleasant way the hospital operated -- anyone could discuss things with the superintendent.

The first year at Ypsilanti was very pleasant, but my drinking was beginning to pick up. I was getting to the point where heavy, nightly drinking was becoming routine for me. By the end of the first year, I was drinking heavily every night -- no longer because I wanted to but because I had to. I was now a drug addict in every sense of the word, and alcohol was my drug. One of my drinking friends was a psychiatrist who was to die not many years later because of his alcoholism.

He and three or four others had an apartment in Ann Arbor over "The Pretzel Bell", a favorite drinking place of the University of Michigan students. Parties were always going on there, and I was always in attendance. My drinking was becoming more uncontrollable.

By now, I was experiencing severe depression, anxiety, vague fears, insomnia, a total lack of confidence, and felt I was losing touch with reality. One might wonder why I didn't think of alcoholism. I can only say that, at that time, an alcoholic was seen as one who was undependable, irresponsible, degenerate, a skid-row person. I clearly was none of these.

My abilities were such that I was in charge of the male service, which meant that administratively I was in charge of half the hospital patients.

Become Annoyed When People Talk to Us About Our Drinking. Frieda, a social worker and friend, told me I was drinking too much, and, of course, I became annoyed with her. There is no doubt she was trying to help me, but she didn't know that one doesn't help the alcoholic by telling him he drinks too much. She was, as I recall, the only one who at least made an effort to help me see my growing problem with alcohol.

Loss of Other Interests. One of my close friends was a psychologist and professional golfer. We had a small nine-hole golf course on the grounds, which gave me an excellent chance to improve my golf. But golf would have interfered with my drinking as would theatre, sightseeing or concerts.

One Sunday afternoon while driving to buy wine, I was arrested and charged with driving under the influence. I spent a night in the Ypsilanti jail, one of the longest nights of my life. The following day in court I was fined, lost my driver's license, and was reprimanded by the judge who asked me how I could let this happen to me considering I was a physician. He must have thought that doctors were immune to becoming alcoholics, or that one day I suddenly decided, "I think I'll become an alcoholic." I'm happy to say that most judges are more enlightened now about alcoholism. In fact, on several occasions, I have told judges I felt that they are responsible for more alcoholics recovering than are doctors. That is because judges are often in a position to give an alcoholic the choice of jail or treatment for alcoholism. If only that option had been offered then, what pain and suffering I might have avoided.

In 1980, I was speaking to a medical group in Baltimore about alcoholism. A doctor I had known during the period when my drinking was out of control came up to me. He said, "Leo, in retrospect, how could we have helped you?" I said, "Why in the name of God did none of you ever come to me and confront me about my alcoholism?" In answer, he actually hung his head. This is no reflection on this doctor because he is one of the kindest, most concerned persons I have ever known; in fact, when I think of my days in Michigan, he is one of the ones I warmly remember. No, this did not reflect on him but upon the ignorance about dealing with the alcoholic -- an ignorance which regrettably is still with us.

After my arrest and the loss of my driver's license, I was more depressed than ever. During that time, none of my co-workers knew how to approach me with any words of comfort; only one person, a patient, was able to show some concern.

Benny, an elderly schizophrenic patient on one of my wards, was very fond of me. The hospital often received tickets for patients to go to concerts in Ann Arbor. Several times I took Benny to concerts. After my involvement with the law, Benny came to me, put his hand on my shoulder and said, "Dr. Leo, everything is going to be all right." I do not feel it at all inappropriate to mention that, thinking of Benny as I am writing this, tears come to my eyes. Several times Benny would tell me about patients who were getting worse and suggest I might have to transfer this patient to a closed ward. I would of course thank him for his concern and look into the situation. Usually, he would be right.

During my second year in Michigan, I lived in Ann Arbor in the shadow of the stadium. In spite of my interest in college football and the reputation of the University of Michigan team, I went to only one game that year. I was drinking more and more and withdrawing more and more. During this time, I often became terrified about losing control of my life, but I did not know what to do about it. Because of my religious background, I turned more and more to religion, but that is not the treatment for alcoholism.

One More Attempt at a Geographical Cure. In 1955, I was toying with the idea of returning to Washington, D.C. and beginning psychotherapy for myself. However, I heard from Dr. Cody, who was with me during the episode with Father J. at St. Elizabeth's. He was leaving his position at the territorial hospital in Hawaii and thought I might be interested in applying. I did apply and was accepted and soon left from Los Angeles on the Lurline, sister ship of the Monterey, on which I went to New Guinea in 1943.

I was still thinking that maybe a move to another place would help to solve some of my problems. I had now finished all my formal training in psychiatry and was a staff psychiatrist at the territorial hospital of Hawaii in Kaneohe on the island of Oahu. During that year, I was also the prison psychiatrist at the Oahu prison. As prison psychiatrist, I would spend Thursday afternoons at the prison seeing prisoners and then go to one of the hotels on Waikiki Beach to eat and drink -- mostly drink. It was probably after one of those drinking sessions, while driving back from Honolulu to Kaneohe, that I hit a telephone pole and spent a night and a day in a hospital. I was driving without a license, since I had never renewed the one I lost in Michigan.

When I arrived in Hawaii, my name and where I came from was in the newspaper, since a new psychiatrist coming to the territorial hospital was considered newsworthy. A man from my part of Pennsylvania, an ex-FBI man, contacted me and we became friends. My accident was reported in the paper. When he found out I was driving without a license, he arranged for me to get one without any problem. When asked by the officer when applying for the license, how much I had drunk, my answer of course was the proverbial, "A few beers." Obviously, this was nowhere near the truth.

Following this incident, I received a very nice letter from a woman who had been a patient at the Territorial Hospital for many years. She expressed her concern for my predicament and offered to help me financially if necessary. It was becoming apparent to me that, although my colleagues were unable to help me, there were always patients who showed concern.

In June 1956, I returned to Washington, D.C., and began living with my sister Helen and my brother-in-law, a clinical psychologist. On October 15, 1956, I began working with the Mental Hygiene Clinic of the Veteran's Administration (VA) in Washington, D.C. When I started, I was the only full-time psychiatrist, and there were four part-time psychiatrists. One year later to the day all four had left and I was in charge of the clinic, which suffered much interdisciplinary friction and was chronically understaffed. We took care of the needs of over a thousand patients, most of them chronic and on tranquilizers; I was the only one who could write prescriptions. Besides this, I was handling all the administrative details and trying to develop the clinic staff into a team.

I began by having a daily staff meeting to give everyone a chance to voice their grievances and suggestions. By helping them to realize we could make our work enjoyable only by working together, we finally achieved a smooth running operation. Staff morale was high and

and we were working together as a team.

One person most helpful to me during my thirteen years there was the Chief Psychologist, Dr. Albert Cornsweet. We soon found we could trust and depend upon each other, and, as time went on, and my alcoholism progressed, he always took over in a calm, uncomplaining way. He was a most important person during those trying years.

As happens when I come to a new place, all goes well for awhile (regarding my drinking). I accept the challenges offered me and do my best when there are serious challenges.

I was in a new relationship with a woman. She was very helpful and understanding about my drinking. She helped me face and conquer one of my many phobias, this one a fear of water. I would not go in water over my waist, but she managed to get me to take swimming lessons. We took a series of ten lessons at the old Ambassador Hotel in Washington. By the end of ten lessons, I progressed to where I could dive off the diving board and swim the length of the pool. Other phobias were not as easily conquered.

I had by now decided I needed help with my problems and consulted with a well-known psychoanalyst in Washington. In spite of my telling him about my drinking escapades, my depression, and my bloated appearance, he never mentioned alcoholism. He referred me to another psychoanalyst. I saw this psychoanalyst once before the annual meeting of the American Psychiatric Association in May 1957 in Chicago. While driving to Chicago, I was arrested for driving at 115 miles per hour. Treatment began when I returned from the meeting.

I began therapy twice a week. This was soon changed to three times a week. At that time, my salary as a full-time psychiatrist was $8,990 a year, and I was paying $20 or $25 a session for treatment. In the initial few years there was no insurance, so I was not exactly living luxuriously. Therapy continued with the first analyst for about six years. We, or rather I, talked about all the members of my family and my relationship to them as well as my other relationships; whenever I had a drinking episode, we would try to determine what it was each time that led to my drinking. This was an exercise in futility. Trying to find a cause for why an alcoholic drinks on each occasion is absurd, for the alcoholic actually drinks for only one reason -- regardless of what reasons he gives, he drinks because he is a drug addict and alcohol is his drug.

Let me say that during 16 years of therapy, no doctor, no therapist, no analyst ever mentioned alcoholism or AA.

When I was a senior in medical school in 1950, Captain George

Raines, Chief Psychiatrist for the Navy and Chairman of Psychiatry at Georgetown University Medical School, mentioned in a lecture his asking a well-known psychiatrist how he dealt with his alcoholics, and was told that he sent them to Alcoholics Anonymous (AA). There were those who at least knew that AA was the proper treatment for alcoholics, but apparently this was not known by my two psychiatrists and the internists I saw in the early 60s.

As I have mentioned, it is fruitless to try to determine why an alcoholic drinks on each occasion. It does no good and, in fact, does harm by creating the illusion that something is being done. In reality nothing is being done by this therapy to help the alcoholic.

I am often asked how I compare psychotherapy with AA as a form of treatment for the alcoholic, and I respond by saying the best answer I can give is to quote Lincoln when he said, "I hope God is on our side but we must have Kentucky." Simply put, if you're an alcoholic, you may need psychotherapy, too, but you must have AA. Only ten to fifteen percent will require psychotherapy as well as AA.

About 1963 I changed therapists because I saw no improvement. During my last visit with my first therapist, I asked if he thought I was an alcoholic, and he said, "Yes, I always felt you were." He had never said this to me, nor had he made any reference to AA. I began therapy with another psychoanalyst which continued until 1973. Both of them have good reputations and probably for other conditions are effective, but their knowledge of alcoholism left much to be desired.

The reader may be saying, Why didn't I know I was an alcoholic, and why didn't I know about AA? The answer is quite simple: I was not the doctor, I was the patient. Why should I, the patient, be expected to make the diagnosis and know the treatment?

I have been asked, if an analyst had recommended AA at any time, would I have gone? At that time, I was indoctrinated into the concept of authority because of my Irish Catholic background -- who was more an authority to a young psychiatrist in those years than psychoanalysts? The answer is an emphatic "yes." I would have done exactly what I was told to do and would have gone to AA.

Let us go back to my being in charge of the Mental Hygiene Clinic, a position which began on October 15, 1957. Then I was the only psychiatrist left. Although my drinking was soon to become more serious, my work was viewed very positively by my supervisors. This is not meant to boast, but to let you know the contrast between my drinking and my career.

Shortly after I became Acting Chief Psychiatrist, I was recommended for a selective promotion, that is, a promotion to a grade higher than warranted by my educational background. The promotion was turned down, but was given to me the following year. During that time I also received several complimentary letters from my supervisors related to my performance.

For awhile I was the only psychiatrist in the clinic and the amount of work was tremendous. Gradually I began to get more help and eventually we had four psychiatrists.

The first one to come spent the first week merely observing; this was my policy for newcomers. After he observed the pace I was setting, he expressed concern to Miriam, a social worker. She reassured him, and correctly so, by saying that I would not expect him to work at my pace. He was a welcome addition to the clinic and is now a good friend of mine.

One night Miriam and I went to a restaurant. I knew that since she was Jewish, she probably would not be accustomed to heavy drinking. Therefore, I drank what I thought was in a moderate manner. Later she told me how concerned she was about the amount I drank, since she didn't see how I could drink that much and drive. I asked her how did I drive, and I believe she said something to the effect that I drove as if I had been drinking water.

We alcoholics can, of course, due to our high tolerance, drink heavily and seem to drive safely, but it is only an illusion. I might have seemed to be in control of my driving, but my reflexes would have been slow. I was not a safe driver and certainly not as much in control as appeared on the surface.

3. DRUGS AND DREAMS

"O' God that men should put an enemy in their mouths to steal away their brains! That we should with joy, pleasance, revel, and applause, transform ourselves into beasts!"
— Othello, Shakespeare

Writing this book has brought back many painful memories, as I force myself to look critically at what was happening to me, particularly during my Veterans Administration (VA) years from 1956 to 1969. For me, one of the most unpleasant side effects of alcohol was my suffering from disturbing dreams. Often I awakened because of them. These dreams are no more.

During the writing of this book, I went to different libraries, including the Library of Congress, American University, Georgetown University, Walter Reed Army Hospital, the National Medical Library, and finally one day, the medical library at the VA hospital. I had, until then, avoided the VA medical library for some time. After I left the VA in 1969, I was unable to return there even to visit friends because it was the site of the worst experiences in my life.

When finally I was able to return for visits, it was often when my life was not going too well. I went back to gain perspective on what I had escaped and how my life had improved. More recently, I found I could hear Mozart's Symphony No. 29 with pleasure, a piece that comforted me in my despair years ago. Now, while driving to the VA, I could listen to it with calm appreciation.

What happened when I first came to the VA is what often happens to an alcoholic engaged in a geographic cure -- temporary improvement. I had returned to D.C. after four years and had a new job; a year later I was in charge of the clinic; I was soon to receive a citation for my work and get a promotion. In addition, I now had a meaningful relationship in my life. Yes, the first few years were interesting and challenging. I was in a position to demonstrate my administrative ability by getting a clinic torn with dissension to work effectively as a team.

I was now working harder at trying to control my drinking, but soon began failing more and more. I tried to minimize my drinking during the week and do most of it on weekends. Perhaps the worst symptom I experienced during those years was insomnia, and, early in treatment with my first psychoanalyst, I asked him to write a prescription for a sedative so I could get some sleep. He responded with, "Why don't you write your own, you're a doctor." I had never considered writing a prescription for myself -- but I did.

I began writing prescriptions for sedatives and getting samples from representatives of drug companies. It wasn't long before I was addicted to drugs. I did not realize this until many years later. With the introduction of pills, I was trying to move from drinking to the use of sedatives in order to deal with my insomnia.

The dosages I recommended for myself were nowhere near the normally accepted amounts. Eventually I developed a pattern of using one sedative for a few months and then changing to another to create the illusion I was not addicted to any one drug. The truth was -- I was addicted to all of them. In my opinion, an alcoholic cannot safely use any mood-changing drugs on an outpatient basis.

Over the years a pattern developed. To deal with my anxiety, I used tranquilizers. To deal with insomnia, I took sedatives. I even used an antihistamine, Benadryl, because of its sedative effect. Then I needed uppers to counteract the downers. My life was controlled by my need for drugs.

During some of the early years, from 1956 to 1960, when I lived in Virginia with my sister and brother-in-law, I would do my drinking in Washington, D.C., often at the Willard Hotel on Pennsylvania Avenue.

There would be days when I would go out to my car to go to work and realize that I remembered drinking in D.C. and getting in my car, but did not remember driving home. There were several occasions when, driving over the 14th Street bridge, I would see two sets of headlights approaching when there was only one car; then I found I could change two sets into one by pressing on the side of my eye. This is a good example of the insanity of alcoholism.

Neglect of Food. I was now beginning to become indifferent to food, and in fact, indifferent to my usual cultural interests.

Onset of Tremors. While still in Virginia, I was beginning to experience shakes and tremors, and discovered the magic of the morning drink to ease these symptoms.

Early Morning Drink. During the last year while living in Virginia, 1956 to 1960, I began to depend on the morning drink. I would have breakfast at a neighborhood restaurant, instead of where I worked, because I wanted to have a beer with breakfast. I was an alcoholic from the onset of my drinking in 1946, but the morning drink did not become a necessity until 1959. It was probably about this time I also became aware of my need to have lunch where I could drink, and it often became my custom to have a few drinks of vodka for lunch.

At this point, the nonalcoholic reader may wonder how could my illness have progressed so far, and yet I was still able to function. The answer is that an alcoholic for many years may have tremendous recuperative powers and may drink heavily at night and, in fact, be in terrible shape, and yet be able to snap back the next morning and function very well. Much of what we do at work, whatever it is, has a routine to it; much of what we do is often done almost without our awareness.

For example, I know of obstetricians delivering babies they later didn't remember delivering; pilots making flights they later didn't remember; a bridge player who was a fellow patient with me at one time winning a tournament he didn't remember being in; a concert pianist giving a concert he later didn't remember. Thus, some of my recollections are hazy.

More than once, someone who worked with me seemed shocked to see me at work and in good condition. When I asked why they were so shocked, this person told me she had talked with me the night before and couldn't believe anyone could change so fast. This is the nature of alcoholism: the alcoholic has a high tolerance for alcohol, but this eventually changes and he can get drunk on less and less alcohol.

By now, all my symptoms were becoming worse -- insomnia, anxiety, depression, tremors, and a generalized fear. In AA, one hears the phrase, "feeling of impending doom," and this is a good description of the fear alcoholics have as our illness progresses.

I was working harder than ever. My routine was becoming more constricted. I was desperately trying to hold onto reality, still believed in the magic of psychoanalysis, and was unable to realize that psychoanalysis for me, at that time, was futile.

Getting to work on time wasn't a problem because alcoholics are notorious about being punctual. I worked very hard seeing large numbers of patients, running the clinic, and dealing, at least in the early years, with some very difficult individuals in the social service department. Fortunately, this was offset by the excellent cooperation of the Psychology Department under Dr. Albert Cornsweet.

At the end of the work day, I was totally exhausted, both because of the work and my severe anxiety; but, as soon as I left the building, much of this tiredness departed.

In 1960, two days after President Kennedy was elected, I moved to the Woodner Apartments on 16th Street, N.W., in Washington, D.C. My place was conveniently located two floors above the cocktail lounge. There, for the next few years, I did much of my drinking. There, I also met two people who were to become two of my closest friends and advisors, Mary Taylor and Claire Poller.

AT WORK

By the end of 1960, I had established an excellent clinic with strong morale, good consultants, and exciting conferences. However, my disease was progressing rapidly. Usually after finishing work, I would eat and begin drinking. Each evening I was obsessed with two concerns: Would I be able to sleep nightmare-free? How much could I drink or use drugs and still be able to get to work in the morning?

The concern about sleep presented me with two choices: If I drank or took drugs in a moderate way, I couldn't sleep, and I would be alone with all my fears and worries; If I took enough alcohol or drugs to sleep, I could be certain to experience terrifying nightmares.

As time went on, I began to have less ability to predict how much I could drink or what amount of drugs I could use, and I began to experience more periods of confusion.

Undefinable Fears. One time I was sleeping on the floor. I could have done so because I had a fear of falling out of bed. I was so drunk, confused, and in such terror, I was afraid I was going to fall off the floor.

Impaired Thinking. Another time, I was awakened at about 4:00 a.m. and imagined a loud noise to be that of Russian planes flying down the street, an incident I described at the beginning of my story.

When I tell these stories in AA, I present them, as we usually do, with some humor (and it can be so in retrospect). However, in order for the reader to experience the terror the alcoholic goes through, I ask you to imagine what you would be experiencing if you were so out of control you feared falling off the floor; if you feared you were psychotic. If your loneliness was so profound, you welcomed the presence of cockroaches. By now, my condition was that severe, and I was living under conditions that are better not described. My feeling of losing touch with reality was so profound and terrifying that there were times I imagined being held by the Blessed Virgin Mary to keep from going totally insane.

Hopelessness. Many times the suffering was unbearable. Because of my feeling of hopelessness, futility, and the feeling that even God had abandoned me, I prayed for death. I had been doing exactly what I was told to do: be treated by a psychoanalyst, but my condition was becoming worse.

Although at times I prayed for death, I was reluctant to do something I thought might help alleviate my depression because it could lead to death. I thought of trying to bring on a grand mal seizure (convulsion) by hyperventilating (rapid deep breathing), because convulsions are known to relieve depression. I had given hundreds of electroshock treatments, but I feared being by myself during a possible seizure (convulsion) because I might swallow my tongue and suffocate.

Even after reading of my experiences, you may be a bit skeptical when I say that, having been a physician in the field of psychiatry for 39 years, I know of no suffering equal to that of the alcoholic and no feeling of loneliness so profound as that of the alcoholic.

At one AA meeting, I said I know of only two things worse than being an alcoholic: knowing the Mafia has a contract on you and being a prisoner in a concentration camp in Nazi Germany. After the meeting, a man came up to me and said, "I was in a concentration camp, and alcoholism is worse."

If the suffering of the alcoholic is so severe, you may wonder why more people are not aware of it. There are four basic reasons:

- *The average person doesn't really see alcoholism as a disease and feels little compassion for the alcoholic's suffering;*
- *The nonalcoholic, accustomed to a joyful experience, or at least no pain from alcohol, can't identify with the alcoholic's suffering.*
- *The alcoholic, knowing he or she will get little sympathy, practically never talks about the severity of his or her suffering before coming to AA;*
- *Experience has taught the alcoholic that to complain is to be told to stop drinking, and this the alcoholic can't do without help.*

It is hard to imagine that a person with such experiences could function at all, but an alcoholic can have a fantastic sense of survival; he or she can make amazing improvement with the sunrise. It is somewhat amusing when people accuse alcoholics of having no will power. I suggest that to experience what I experienced at night and still do the quality and quantity of work I did for years requires will power.

If you are skeptical, as a nonalcoholic, try drinking a fifth of whiskey some evening; go to work the next day and try to do your job well.

Telephonitis. Another definite symptom of alcoholism, related to our profound feeling of loneliness, is the use of the telephone. We often call people from our distant past. It can of course be somewhat indiscreet, to say nothing of being dangerous to one's health, to call old girl friends of 10 to 15 years ago. When loneliness was profound, I called information and asked the telephone number of the Smithsonian Institution at 3:00 a.m., just to hear a human voice.

Some years ago I was visiting someone at the Woodner in the coffee shop when I ran into a friend who knew me during my drinking years. He told me of an incident that had him puzzled. He said that some woman he barely knew called him while she was under the influence of alcohol. They had been at a party about five years previously and he had merely met her. I explained to him that, as our alcoholism progresses, we often have no good human experiences for years. To capture a good one, we have to go back in time to do so. I said, "You may have shown some kindness to her, or some understanding which no one else did, and now years later, and drinking, she remembers you with some positive feeling." Usually these calls are early in the morning. Another time he told me about a friend who had moved to Florida and would call him once or twice a year, usually about 2:00 or 3:00 a.m. I explained that his friend was probably an alcoholic. I believe that if all alcoholics were to recover suddenly, the phone company would lose a great deal of money.

Missing Work on Mondays. About this time, I was beginning to find my weekends were getting longer, and I began missing work on Mondays. It has been said, "Don't buy a car that comes off the assembly line on Mondays." As I began to note my poor performance on Mondays, I would reschedule my Monday therapy patients to another day.

At sometime in the very early 60s, I began not trusting my driving and would go to work by bus or cab. I also began to doubt my ability to determine whether or not I was fit to work, and therefore arranged to meet with a social worker before work. We would meet in the cafeteria; she would observe me, talk with me, and would often tell me I shouldn't be working. I always accepted her judgment, and if she said no, I would return home.

I wondered if it would be advisable for me to become a staff psychiatrist and give up being Acting Chief Psychiatrist. I discussed it with my analyst and when he agreed that I should do so, I gave up the Acting Chief position. I later realized that one should never do this in any work situation. Maintain your position, go higher, or leave.

We then had a psychoanalyst in charge of the clinic who, although a very brilliant and wonderful person, was quite disturbed because of his manic-depressive illness. The result was I had to do my work and help him, and take over the clinic whenever he was hospitalized, which was often.

One of my patients, Harry, a schizophrenic, was very perceptive about my growing problems with alcohol and with the new administration. He was a legend around the clinic. He became fond of me, very protective, and often asked me to visit him if I ever happened to be in Alexandria, Virginia. Now and then, Harry would call me at home to see how I was doing. Apparently one time I didn't sound too well, so he called a close friend of mine then in Maine, saying, "Ruth, Doc's not doing so well; I think you should get down here." I believe I noted more concern over the years from the patients I treated than from the professionals with whom I worked.

TREATMENT CENTERS

In 1962, I was being treated for hypertension by a leading internist in Washington, D.C. I saw him but a few times and was then referred to a colleague of his. At this time, Capt. Harold Roche and Frances (my childhood friend Joe's sister) helped me by having me stay at their home for a period of time. My condition was becoming worse. I was subsequently hospitalized on February 16, 1963, with the diagnosis of acute anxiety reaction. My admission note states:

> *The patient is a 41-year-old white male psychiatrist who has been bothered by anxiety and nervous tension for the last three to four years with insomnia, excessive alcoholic intake, and increased sedative ingestion. Presently the patient has had a marked increase in symptoms associated with unfavorable news regarding his best friend, colleague, and boyhood chum. Insomnia has increased, as has alcohol ingestion to a fifth per day, with time lost from work, decreased appetitie and weight loss. Blood pressure is 180/115 and patient shows chronic depressive reaction -- agitated with alcoholic excess.*

Most interesting about all of this is that in spite of the fact that the record shows excess use of alcohol and sedatives, at no time was it discussed with me, and no one saw fit to have me seen by a consultant who was qualified to deal with alcoholism and drug addiction. I was discharged on February 21, 1963.

In the spring of 1963 something happened that finally led me in the direction of getting well. A friend of mine who then worked at the VA, Pete Sterrantino, told me he heard rumors about the possibility of my being fired. It was then I called AA and before long had a call from Dr. Joe C. I believe that Joe has probably been responsible for more physicians recovering from alcoholism and drug addiction in the Washington, D.C. area than any other person, physician or not. At that moment did I know I was an alcoholic? Did I want to give up alcohol forever? The answer was "no" to both questions. I had two goals in mind when I called AA: I wanted to get six months of sobriety and I wanted to make my job more secure.

That evening Joe arrived in his Kharmann Ghia. As we drove to the meeting he didn't ask me much about myself or alcohol or drugs, but I suspect he knew by looking at me why I had called AA. Joe didn't ask much about me, but he told me a lot about himself. For the first time in all those years, I felt accepted, and, as Joe eventually pointed out, I wasn't weak or immoral -- I had a sickness called alcoholism. There wasn't much he hadn't done regarding alcohol and drugs of every description: time in mental hospitals, losing his license to practice medicine. I began to feel like Little Lord Fauntleroy by comparison.

Sick as I was, I was not without compassion for Joe, because I remember thinking (but not saying), "Thank God this poor devil's in AA; he really needs it." I was, of course, doing what alcoholics and drug addicts often do: we try to deny our alcoholism and drug addiction by comparing ourselves with someone else and noting how much worse someone else's illness is.

I don't remember who spoke at the AA meeting or too much about it, except that for the first time in many years, I experienced hope. I had all but given up on numerous occasions. I had thought AA was a place for skidrow people; that it consisted of someone getting up and saying, "I used to be a sinner and drank two fifths a day, and then I found God." Well, it was not like that. There was no talk of sin; people seemed happy. When they told me what they had done with alcohol and drugs and how they were now happy, I must admit I was a bit skeptical, but it seemed worth trying. Most important was that people accepted me, seemed to care, and said something I had not heard in years, "Please come back."

It would be nice if I could say I became immediately involved in AA and never drank or used drugs again, but unfortunately that was not so. I went to an occasional meeting and tried to do what they said: don't drink -- one day at a time. I did go six months without a drink.

For the first time in many years, I was beginning to feel like a human being; the change was dramatic. I noted it; others noticed it. My level of anxiety and depression was much lower; I began to like myself; but sleep still presented a major problem.

Decrease in Alcohol Tolerance. Since I had not had a vacation in years, I decided it was time for one. I decided to go to Puerto Rico and the Virgin Islands for 10 days. I was new at AA so I had not yet learned that vacations are very dangerous for alcoholics. Soon I was to discover it to be so.

On the plane I was asked if I wanted a drink. Apparently I said yes because I remember little else about the rest of the vacation. That evening in the dining room in Puerto Rico, I remember a pianist playing a favorite song of mine, "La Comparsa," by Ernesto Leucona, and I remember going to the Virgin Islands where I bought five fifths. This, plus returning to D.C., is all I remember of those 10 days.

There was a time during my drinking when I looked forward to Fridays so I could "enjoy" drinking. I would buy whatever I would want to drink. By now it was wine because I could no longer judge the amount of alcohol I could consume and wine gave me more control. I would select the books to read, usually something very pictorial because my vision would soon show the effects of the drinking, and I would be off in a world of fantasy.

Drinking for Oblivion. I could in fantasy be a composer, conductor, concert pianist, anything I wanted -- but eventually even this stopped being pleasurable. All reality was painful; my drinking now was to achieve oblivion.

I don't remember how long I continued to drink before I returned to AA, probably a few months. I believe I became a bit more involved this time and had a longer period of sobriety. It may have been the next drinking episode that led to my being admitted to a drying out place in Washington, D.C., called Kalorama, which in Greek means "beautiful view." To me it was reminiscent of Charles Dickens' stories. In those days, hospitals didn't accept alcoholics, so one got in wherever your friends could get you in; you were dried out for a few days, and then literally pushed out the door.

At the end of my few days there, I knew I couldn't work, knew I couldn't go back to my apartment, and knew I was in serious trouble.

Some friends found a place for me in Paterson, New Jersey run by the Catholic Church. It was called Mt. Carmel, a place for alcoholics and drug addicts.

The arrangements were as follows: From the train station in Washington, D.C., I was to go to the New York Port Authority and wait at a certain pillar where I would be picked up by a stranger and taken to Mt. Carmel.

Even now the words "New York" cause me apprehension and it was no different then. However, I did get to the station, managed not to drink on the train, and got to my destination. I was met by this stranger from AA and taken to Mt. Carmel. I do not mean any offense to the state of New Jersey, but Paterson seemed to be about the worst place I had ever seen. Mt. Carmel was in Paterson's warehouse district located at the corner of Straight Street and Narrow Street. For years I felt I must have had brain damage to imagine such an address.

It was like living in a barracks. I worked at some type of press involved in binding magazines and papers. It was the hardest job, physically, I had ever done, but it was not all without reward, because at the end of the week I was paid $1.00 -- not $1.00 an hour, but for a week! In 1980, when I was visiting my sister Mary in New Jersey, I went back to Mt. Carmel to see if it was as bad as I remembered it. It was. I checked the street signs at the location -- still Straight and Narrow. I am not critical of Mt. Carmel, because at least they took me in when no other place would and they tried. I stayed there about 10 days during which, I had a grand mal seizure, and then returned to work at the clinic.

Over those years I made attempts to get off alcohol and instead use drugs for sedation; but after taking a few pills (no alcoholic ever takes one of anything), I could easily become confused as to how much I took and also when I took it. When you are alone and lonely, a minute can seem like an eternity and it is easy to become confused in these matters. In general, however, I was taking placidyl and would routinely take three capsules of 500 milligrams. For a period, I was not drinking but was taking sodium amytal at night. I would routinely take three 3-grain capsules, and seemed to be managing better than when drinking or using other sedatives. Placidyl, in my opinion, is the more dangerous.

On December 27, 1964, I was admitted to Georgetown Hospital with the diagnoses of overdose of Placidyl and chronic alcoholism. The admission note states:

> *Forty-three year old white male psychiatrist admitted in semistuporous state. Known to be a heavy drinker and was found in his apartment with many empty bottles. Possible history of seizure in the past. On discharge from the hospital, he developed a possible seizure and was readmitted. . Patient is an alcoholic psychiatrist, blood pressure 180/130.*

A few days after admission, I was discharged and within a few minutes, I had a grand mal seizure and was readmitted, to be discharged on January 2, 1965. I remember walking out of the hospital with my sister and brother-in-law and getting in the car. The next thing I remembered was looking at the ceiling in the emergency room. Obviously, I had been discharged prematurely.

I was evaluated by cardiologists and neurologists, but despite my history and the dual diagnosis on my chart, no one talked about alcoholism or drug addiction or even seemed concerned about these conditions.

On April 22, 1965, I was readmitted to the same hospital, by the same doctor, to be studied for the causes of hematuria. My opinion as to its cause was that I probably hurt myself when I fell while under the influence of alcohol or drugs.

My doctor decided I should have a kidney biopsy, since he suspected a collagen disease. A collagen disease is one of several diseases of the connective tissue and is usually fatal -- at least it was then. My medical record states: "Collagen disease a likely cause -- feel that renal biopsy indicated." On April 25, 1965, the medical record indicates: "Patient seen by Dr. X. Feels biopsy at present not indicated." Dr. X. was head of the nephrology department. My memory is that I was minutes from going to the operating room for biopsy when Dr. X. happened by and began to question what was going on.

Another note in my record shows: "[Patient] up and walking about. Continues to be very nervous and jumpy." I'm sure it was not without good reason. After cancellation of the biopsy, I experienced great fear. A noted doctor tells me I probably have a collagen disease, but then a biopsy is cancelled. I thought that my disease had already gone too far to justify a biopsy. I saw the doctor some years ago, not professionally but in passing, and I had the distinct feeling he was surprised to see me still among the living. Of course, I could have read that into his expression. One may safely assume his diagnosis was incorrect as evidenced by the fact that I'm still alive. I didn't get well because of my doctors, but in spite of them.

4. TOWARD RECOVERY

"No grand Inquisitor has in readiness such terrible torture as anxiety."

— Soren Kierkegaard

When I now tell my story in AA, I say that from 1963 until April 1967, I was an associate member of AA and each episode of drinking (in AA we call it "research") was followed by a slightly longer period of sobriety. Sometime in April 1967, while on vacation, I went to the cocktail lounge of the Woodner and had about seven cocktails. The following night I had five, and the night after that, three. Fortunately, I saw what I was up to -- pretending I was cutting down! I might say here the alcoholic mind takes great liberty with logic. I called Dr. Frank Cresswell, whom I had met through a friend. I asked him if he thought I could benefit from being on Antabuse. He thought I might, and I began taking Antabuse and took it for six years until about 1973 when I felt I could trust myself.

What was I up to regarding the seven, five, and three cocktails? I was trying to convince myself I wasn't an alcoholic, since my drinking decreased two nights in a row. Why did I stop then and not a year or two sooner, or for that matter, a year or two later? I really don't know. I suppose I finally got completely honest with myself regarding my relationship with alcohol. I don't remember the exact date of my last drink. In AA it helps us to have specific dates; my brother Paul's birthday was April 11 and I remember April 11, 1967, as the day of my last drink.

About the time I was getting off alcohol (1966 to 1967) I met Ruth, who was in AA and who, according to her, was alive only because of Dr. Cresswell. She told me of the time she had a ruptured cerebral aneurysm, and her friend Lucia, a nurse, got her to Dr. Cresswell. Ruth believes that, with her history of alcoholism, many doctors would have felt she was drunk and would have missed the diagnosis. Dr. Cresswell not only made the correct diagnosis, but took her to Dr. Rizzoli, one of the best neurosurgeons in the city, and Ruth made a good recovery.

Ruth smoked more than anyone I ever knew. Considering most members of AA are heavy smokers, you can imagine her addiction. One night in her apartment where I had taken Valium and was a bit shaky on my feet, I heard Ruth scream. When I turned around Ruth's bathrobe was going up in flames. In spite of my condition, I grabbed a blanket, wrapped it around Ruth, dragged her to more blankets on the bed, and got the fire out. I later told Ruth that was the fastest I ever got a woman into bed. She was severely burned but didn't want to bother any doctor at that time of night and insisted upon waiting until the next morning. Tragically, a few years ago while she was in Maine, the diagnosis of cancer of the lung was made, and she was told it was inoperable. She came to Washington to see Dr. Cresswell who arranged an appointment for her with a local thoracic surgeon. I saw Ruth on the Thursday after her appointment, and we went to a favorite AA meeting of hers, ate in a favorite Chinese restaurant of ours, and visited some of her friends. I was to meet Ruth Saturday and we were to visit more of her friends, most of them in AA. When I went to pick her up at Lucia's at noon Saturday, Lucia told me Ruth had died during the night. Ruth, an unusually kind, gentle person, helped me a great deal and also helped many others.

From 1963 (when I joined AA) to April 1967 when I had my last drink, I had many periods of abstinence from alcohol, and many periods when I seemed to use drugs more cautiously. I seemed to be improving.

During this time I found that I had been considered for my next promotion, based on years of service. My promotion wasn't discussed with me, and I was turned down several times. This was contrary to VA policy, particularly since each year I received notification that my work was satisfactory.

In 1963, when the clinic was still located at 21st Street and Constitution Avenue, I was transferred from the Mental Hygiene Clinic to the Medical Clinic after a drinking episode. Again, no one confronted me about my alcoholism. Although I had had nothing to do with physical medicine since I finished my internship in 1952, I was expected to examine patients and prescribe accordingly. No one told me why I was transferred or what the rationale was; I was merely called in to face several sternfaced, angry doctors and told I was being transferred. No explanation was given.

During all my years at the VA, I had one possession that meant much to me, a reclining chair, and I sat in it as I saw my patients. I never saw patients from behind a desk; in fact, I chose not to have a desk in my office. Once when I returned to work from sick leave, my chair was missing. It had been put where I could not get to it -- in the ladies room.

To return again to 1968: having stopped drinking and having a period of drug use that was moderate for me, there was a definite change in my life and my work. A new ward for alcoholics was being opened and I was asked to be in charge. The problem I faced was that I detested the work situation, but knew I was improving physically. Also, I had been there twelve years, so the likelihood of being fired was remote. In those days one could, and often did, lose one's job because of alcoholism. Were this to happen, my situation would have been grim, because I had saved nothing and was living from paycheck to paycheck.

On the other hand, I would have liked a new challenge. I always did my best with new challenges, but I feared that if anything went wrong, I would be in a very vulnerable position. I discussed this with others and the general consensus was that I should take the job with the alcoholic ward if I were given the long-withheld promotion.

When I was called in to meet with those in charge, they were surprised and obviously angry that I made my promotion a condition of being in charge of a new ward. This created more pressure on me.

Soon after that, I went to Boston to attend the annual meetings of the American Psychiatric Association (APA) and met my very close friend, Dr. Ray Hayes. Ray was the superintendent of the Central State Hospital in Louisville, Kentucky, and we arranged then that I visit him.

At this point I would have done anything to get out of the VA in Washington. I was willing to leave and in doing so to give up my government retirement which totaled 18 years. I went to Kentucky, and Ray's good common sense kept me from leaving the VA.

He did arrange for me to meet friends at the Louisville VA Hospital; they were interested in me. However, for whatever reason or reasons, shortly after I returned to D.C., I began using drugs excessively and a friend took me to see Dr. Cresswell. He soon made a recommendation that was to change the course of my life. Dr. Cresswell is not only an expert in the field of alcoholism and drug addiction, but is an outstanding physician in every way. Previously, I had a medical condition, unrelated to alcoholism, that had been misdiagnosed and incorrectly treated, but Dr. Cresswell correctly diagnosed and treated me.

We talked about drugs and alcohol, and since I had no trouble accepting my alcoholism, I asked him if he thought I was a drug addict, and he said, "Leo, all I know is that, whenever you start using drugs, it's usually only a matter of time before you have some difficulty, often ending up in a hospital, unconscious or close to it." He said, "You can call your condition anything you want, but you and drugs are not like ham and eggs." I got the message.

One Wednesday evening I went to the pharmacy at the Woodner, where I lived, to refill a prescription. It was refused because of my condition. I decided then it was a good time to get off drugs and took nothing Wednesday, Thursday, or Friday. On Saturday I felt so good I decided to do what I often do when I feel good -- go for a ride. I drove to Annapolis and, as I was driving around the circle, I began to experience a strange dizzy feeling. I then had a unique experience, one I have never had before or since. I remained completely conscious but had absolutely no control of my muscles. I wanted to steer the car and lift my foot to use the brake, but couldn't. I fell toward the passenger side of the car, and the car, going 5 to 10 miles per hour, came to rest on the curb. I was kept in the hospital a few hours, then discharged. I hired two cab drivers to drive me and my car back to D.C. If it had happened fifteen minutes earlier, I would have been on the highway.

DEALING WITH FEARS

Before I move on to the beginning of my recovery from drug addiction in 1968 (I had now been alcohol-free since 1967), I would like to tell you more about some fears I had from childhood into my mid-40s, and how I began dealing with them.

One was the fear of talking in front of a group of people, another the fear of death. Three things helped me deal with my first fear, the fear of public speaking: I took the Dale Carnegie course, I began giving talks at AA meetings, and I was instructed in public speaking by Pat Sawyer, an actress and public speaking teacher. I no longer have a fear of public speaking.

I had a fear of death from early childhood: one of my first memories is of a small white coffin. My youngest brother died in infancy. I have no doubt that my fear of death had much to do with my insomnia, which I had for about 16 years, because, during my worst years, I feared dying in my sleep. Nothing seemed to help me get over this fear until one night I decided, in sheer desperation, to try something so terrifying that as I write about it, I wonder how I thought of it. This was at a time I often wished I could have a mild heart attack, so people would at least see me as having a legitimate and acceptable illness. Also, having thought about it, I wonder how I was able to do it. When we are desperate enough, we will try anything. That night I decided to face my own death.

I was in bed lying on my back when I forced myself to imagine my death and every aspect of it. I imagined the coffin, the funeral, and all the rituals associated with it including the people who were the pallbearers, and everything else about it. My fear of death left me never to return.

Later, I was somewhat pleased to find that certain religious orders used this principle. I thought how nice it would have been, how much suffering I could have avoided, if this had ever been part of my earlier psychotherapy.

RECOVERING FROM DRUG ADDICTIONS

Now let us get on to matters which, despite a few interruptions, were to lead to my recovery from my drug addictions. Sometime in 1968, Dr. Cresswell convinced me that I needed detoxification as the result of my drug use. I had been using drugs excessively, which is why I came to his attention, thanks to Ruth. Dr. Cresswell prescribed a four-to-six-week hospitalization at an appropriate institution for alcoholism and drug addiction. He had me admitted to Mar Salle near Dupont Circle in Northwest, Washington, D.C.

When I entered Mar Salle, I was very confused and quite depressed and beginning to wonder if I was ever going to make it. I had been in psychotherapy since 1957, in AA since 1963, off alcohol since 1967, and here in 1968 I was in the depths of despair. What I didn't realize then was that I had never dealt with my drug addiction because I never really knew I was a drug addict. Until I met Dr. Cresswell, no doctor of mine knew it either, or, if they knew, they didn't know what to do about it.

As fortune or misfortune would have it, there was a very attractive young female patient there who managed to convince me it would be a sign of maturity if I signed out from Mar Salle against medical advice.

At this point, I was still desperately lonely and responded to the interest of another human. Thus, despite the pleading of the doctor on duty, Nancy and I signed out against medical advice.

Several years ago, this "on duty" doctor was at an AA meeting. I approached him and told him how pleased I was to see him coming to AA to learn more about it. "No, Leo," he said, "I just joined AA a few months ago." Several weeks later Nancy, he, and I were at the same AA meeting and had quite a few laughs recalling the 1968 episode.

To put it very charitably, Nancy was not too tightly wrapped, which is not to imply that I was. That night after we had left a restaurant, where she had been drinking, she was reciting poems and was trying to jump out of the car while I was driving. The scene was reminiscent of an Alfred Hitchcock movie. I got lost, and was driving around in a predominantly black section. The time was shortly after the race riots of the late 60s, and driving a car with a disturbed woman trying to jump out in a black section was not conducive to tranquility. Finally, I became oriented and we went back to her place.

Fortunately, the next day, Dr. Cresswell managed to convince Nancy to drive me to a treatment center, Melwood Farm in Olney, Maryland, and we arrived there on a Wednesday evening just as their lecture was beginning. As if I didn't feel badly enough, my situation was aggravated by the fact that the doctor who was talking to the patients that night was a doctor who interned with me in 1951 at St. Elizabeth's Hospital. One never knows, however, how events will turn out because years ago, as a member of the Committee for the Rehabilitation of Physicians, I made a call on him and he was a member of AA. As for me, I still drive out to visit Melwood Farm several times a year because it represents the beginning of a new life for me.

When I arrived at Melwood Farm, I experienced a new kind of fear -- a realistic one. For years, in fact since 1952, I had depended upon something to help me sleep, alcohol or various drugs in various combinations, and had fixed in my mind the belief that I could not sleep without chemical assistance. I had tried on many occasions to sleep without alcohol or drugs, and the only result was a very bad experience, no sleep or poor sleep. The other choice was to use alcohol or drugs and experience severe nightmares.

I heard others say I could learn to sleep normally, but frankly I didn't believe it. This left me with the conviction that, if I couldn't sleep without alcohol or drugs, I would use them, and probably some night would die of an accidental overdose.

I pondered all this the first two days, and, at night, was given something for sedation. By Friday night I had come to a decision. I had to do whatever had to be done to learn to sleep normally, whatever the cost was in terms of sleeping time or suffering, because I couldn't go on this way.

I never experienced the same fears or difficulty regarding alcohol because I had been able to give up alcohol for periods of time - like so many Irish Catholic alcoholics do during Lent's forty days to prove they are not alcoholics. I had gone for six months without alcohol my first time in AA, but getting off drugs was a different matter.

The first problem I had to deal with was guilt at being there, knowing I would be there for six weeks. I finally was able to accept the fact that I was desperately sick and needed the treatment.

I had a conversation with myself and asked what Dale Carnegie might say about a long stay at Melwood. He might ask, "What's the worst that could happen?" I decided the worst would be losing my job; soon I accepted that maybe that could be a blessing in disguise. Then I asked myself what could I do about my many problems -- job, income tax, poor interpersonal relations, debts. I decided I could do nothing about any of them for six weeks; that the next six weeks were a time devoted to recovering from drug addiction.

COMPLETE DEFEAT -- SURRENDER

Within a week at Melwood, I was becoming a totally different person. My symptoms of depression, anxiety, and insomnia were abating, but there was still fear of the future.

Meeting fellow alcoholics and drug addicts from all walks of life with diverse experiences made my stay there a pleasant experience, one which I shall always remember. It was run by Mary Bacon, a kind, wonderful, bright woman, who ran the place with quiet dignity.

The first night without drugs, I went to bed and prayed to God to help me. When I said the Lord's Prayer and came to "Thy will be done," I began to block on it and started bargaining with God. Part of me was saying, "Not this time, Leo, no bargaining; it must be a total surrender, a total acceptance." But part of me, though believing in God, was fearful because as I looked upon my life, there was little reason to believe God was on my side. Finally, I was able to say, "Leo, you've been trying to run your life as best you can and the results have been none too good -- how can it be worse?" I finally was able simply to ask God's help with no strings attached.

As I tried to sleep, I imagined all my problems in a bag and as they floated toward me, I simply pushed them away. I tried to sleep in bed, tried to sleep on the floor. Then I tried reading and finally I got to sleep close to dawn.

The next night I was determined not to give up and it was similar to the first night, but the third night something different happened. It seemed that as soon as I went to bed, I went into a peaceful sleep such as I had not experienced in sixteen years. For the first time in all those years I slept without alcohol or drugs, but what was perhaps more important, my dreams were peaceful and calm, not filled with fear and terror.

In my dreams I seemed to be moving in space -- going wherever I wanted -- over mountains -- between mountains. I felt I was at peace with the universe and myself. When I awakened in the morning, I thought: Would I take a million dollars for that night's sleep? Immediately I answered out loud, "No."

After thanking God for this experience, I wondered if this was a fluke; but it wasn't. Something very profound had happened, something beyond my wildest expectations, because for the rest of my time at Melwood Farm, I experienced no difficulty in sleeping.

Something else occurred which I never experienced before or since. When I went to bed, I could clearly remember my dreams and how they ended and I was able to continue a dream where it had ended the previous night.

I do not know how to explain what happened in Melwood Farm, but I do know it was an important and dramatic experience. While at Melwood, I was reading a book by Solzhenitsyn, *The First Circle*; a theme in it impressed me so much that I decided to incorporate it into my philosophy of life. The character, a prisoner in Russia, was so punished and brutalized, he felt there could be nothing more they could do to him; he had, he felt, already experienced the maximum amount of suffering. He was then ordered to complete a certain task in a given time. When he evaluated this task, he realized it was impossible to complete it in that given time. Having suffered the maximum, he decided no one could hurt him again. Thus, he felt he could take a stand on the impossibility of the task given him and he so stated.

It was there in Melwood I decided that nothing worse than what had already happened to me could ever happen again. I had experienced the worst. No one could ever again inflict such pain on me -- either by commission or omission.

Because of my poor self image, it was my perception that the medical profession disliked psychiatrists, alcoholics, and drug addicts, and I was all three. I was never really involved with my colleagues. I had only a token membership in medical societies. This was, of course, the fault of no physician or physicians, or any medical society, as any rejection I felt was not based on reality, but was related to how I felt about myself.

On a strictly intellectual level, I knew I was a sick person and not an evil person; but being a product of the attitudes of my culture regarding alcoholics and drug addicts, I usually experienced guilt about my condition.

At times my feeling of despair and worthlessness was so profound that I wanted to apologize to the world for taking up space.

In spite of all this, I somehow clung to a belief that some day, some way, it would all work out.

On a more pleasant note, I experienced a new feeling. My first reaction was, "Oh, God, what now?", for I remembered my experiences with depression, anxiety, and insomnia However, when I calmed down, I was able to identify this new feeling -- it was a feeling of happiness. I had had so little experience with happiness that it had become foreign to me. From that point on, there were major improvements; I knew then that I was capable of feeling good, and that I didn't have to settle for merely not hurting.

During my first visit to Melwood in 1968, I reviewed my life, what I started with, what I had gone through, and what I had conquered. I felt that there was only one direction I could go -- and that was up! At this point, my main concern was whether or not I could get off drugs and then stay off drugs.

Now, at the VA, my old boss had left, and in his stead was a very wonderful person, Dr. Orlando Moreno. As soon as could be arranged, which was about ten months, I was promoted. To say that, of my thirteen years at the VA, seven or eight were absolute hell is to put it mildly.

I had been very, very sick for many years and now that I was alcohol and drug-free and had received my promotion, my job was safe. I was now able to look at how I had been treated -- not with fear but with anger at what had been done to me. Anger because I had been allowed to suffer, and hate for those who never once came to me and asked, "Leo, how can we help you?" Why, during those years, didn't one of my superiors do anything about consulting with an authority in the field of alcoholism and drug addiction?

I had still not learned how to relinquish my hate. Of course, holding on to hate can only lead to disaster and it did.

Several weeks after I received my promotion, I was back on drugs and back to Melwood Farm for the second time.

I don't believe it can ever be called "a slip", as we say in AA; the truth is, I felt I was being destroyed by the job; the amount of work I was doing was far beyond what I had ever done in any work situation. It is not uncommon for some persons to take advantage of an alcoholic's position, and this had happened to me.

Could they not see that punishing a person as they did by withholding my promotion, which was actually a routine matter, was merely driving me deeper into my depression? Obviously they didn't.

On practically every case I know, the employer has been most fair in dealing with alcoholics, in fact often too fair -- to the point of not confronting the alcoholic about his illness. In my case, I experienced fairness and kindness in Connecticut, Michigan, Hawaii, and at the VA for the first few years. It was only during a later period of time that I had employers who were quite vindictive.

It was my feeling that if I remained on that job, I would eventually die of a heart attack.

I wanted to "get even" with the VA, a very immature attitude that cost me dearly. Had I kept my wits about me, I would have simply transferred to another agency.

The tragedy was that no one knew how to deal with an alcoholic psychiatrist, and there I was, surrounded by doctors, psychologists, and social workers.

If I were to be asked how I would best describe myself, I believe I would say that I'm a survivor. I survived a number of incompetent doctors, one of whom told me I had a fatal collagen disease. I survived sixteen years of inept psychotherapy. I survived not only two terrifying diseases, but treatment by several doctors who were not just indifferent but actually cruel.

Later, I was to learn more about forgiveness, not for the sake of my enemies, but because of what hate was doing to me. One dramatic lesson: When I couldn't sleep one morning and was having a fantasy concerning how much the Mafia would charge to make my boss part of the freeway, it suddenly occurred to me that the bastard was probably sleeping soundly and my hate was upsetting me, giving him control over me. It was then I began slowly to forgive him for his ineptness and harassment.

I left the VA on a medical retirement in 1969 with mixed feelings. On one hand, I was being freed from a chamber of horrors, and, on the other hand, I was bitter that my situation was dealt with so poorly. I was trying desperately for years to get well, and I would have done it sooner if I had had the least amount of understanding from my superiors.

The three years after my second stay at Melwood Farm were important years (1969-1972). I had retired from the VA, was feeling good, and thought I was really on my way.

From the time I finished college in January 1946, there had been no let up for me except for the months between my discharge from the army and my entering medical school. The time in the army, most of it in the southwest Pacific, was followed by hard years in medical school. From medical school (1946) until I joined AA in 1963, each year had become progressively worse. There were, of course, many severely disturbing times from 1963 until I opened my office in December 1969.

During these years, vacations were none too many. When I was on one, it was often a time of feeling more unhappy; that's because many of us with severe emotional problems imagine that everyone else is having a much better time.

I review this to emphasize how chronic were my illnesses, particularly my alcoholism and drug addiction, and my myriad of worsening neurotic problems.

When we alcoholics finally do start getting well, we are very, very sick in all categories and are far sicker than we appear on the outside. We are drained physically, emotionally, and spiritually. We have in a sense been in combat for many years and often require a great deal of time before we are completely healed.

STARTING OVER

When I opened my office at 3000 Connecticut Avenue, N.W., Washington, D.C., in December 1969, it was a new beginning.

It appeared that I had finally conquered alcoholism, drug addiction, insomnia, my fear of death and of public speaking, and was slowly but surely beginning to like myself.

Those few months after my discharge from the army and before starting medical school were very joyful months, but other than that my life had been a very unhappy, neurotic one, which became worse as my alcoholism and drug addiction progressed.

When I entered AA and for many years to follow, I was willing to settle merely for the absence of pain. It was inconceivable that I could experience sustained happiness because such had never been the case in my life. To be sure, there were moments of joy, but they were usually separated by longer periods of pain.

I was now free from both drugs and alcohol, but there was still much to be done in terms of changing my overall personality.

Having come from a family where compliments were rare and criticism was common, I had all my life experienced feelings of worthlessness and low self-esteem. For a long time, I felt that practically anyone could become a doctor if he or she really wanted to, because if I could do it anyone could.

Starting off with these feelings and then experiencing what I did while fighting my addictions, one can see why I became guarded and sensitive not only to criticism, but even disagreement from others.

I was careful about taking sides in any discussion because it meant having someone disagree with me; to me this meant not being accepted by them, and disliked. I tried to adopt a middle-of-the-road policy about most matters and, of course, this led to my never having the courage of my convictions. A friend helped me see this when she told me that, rather than take a stand, I would be inclined to adopt a position of, "It's hard to say."

As the reader has perceived, or will perceive by the time you finish this book, this is no longer the case. Since in adopting new beliefs or changing attitudes, we are often like a pendulum. I moved from not taking a stand on anything to taking a strong stand on many issues.

Now that my alcoholism and drug addiction were dealt with, or I should say, almost dealt with (I was to have one more episode in 1972), I still had much work to do on my underlying problems, and I had other problems which had developed during my alcoholism and drug addiction. However, I was hopeful.

Increased Feeling of Hope - The First Sign of Recovery. What happened at Melwood Farm in 1968 was a turning point; it was of a different magnitude than getting off alcohol.

It seems that once I joined AA and began to achieve some sobriety, there was never the same doubt about getting off alcohol that I had concerning drugs.

My concern regarding drugs had to do with my fear of insomnia. Insomnia is a terrifying experience to have night after night, week after week, month after month, year after year, for about sixteen years. To demonstrate to yourself how unpleasant it is, try to stay awake all night for just one night. When I was in the army, one of the men in my outfit came home late one night, made a lot of noise, and awakened most of us. The following night, it was arranged that, every fifteen minutes, someone aroused him. Neither he nor anyone else repeated his performance.

When my Washington office opened, life began to have meaning. In addition, the place where I had been a patient in 1968 and 1969, Melwood Farm, now, in 1970, asked me to be a consultant.

5. STARTING AGAIN AND BACKSLIDING

"I am dying with the help of too many physicians."
— Alexander the Great

From December of 1969 until the end of 1972, for once in my life, I wasn't involved in something frantic. I was receiving a modest pension from the federal government, seeing not too many patients, and, in general, enjoying a tremendous amount of time to do whatever I chose within the limits of my money.

One danger faced me, a danger that faces many improved alcoholics. It is called good health! It often happens to alcoholics, and it happened to me, that the change was so dramatic, life was now so peaceful, so enjoyable, that I forgot, or became less aware of the fact that I had a chronic illness which required ongoing treatment. I forgot how bad it had been; I forgot how necessary it was for me to maintain ongoing treatment; and I began drifting away from AA. At no time did I ever say I didn't need AA; I merely became so absorbed in so many things that I got careless and started going to fewer and fewer AA meetings.

Sometime in 1972, I had a romantic involvement which created some stress. This led to a recurrence of my insomnia, and I wrote a prescription for myself for placidyl. I began using more sedatives and sleeping at my office. One morning, when I looked for my car, I couldn't find it despite a lot of searching, particularly around drug stores, by Dave K., my AA sponsor at that time, and me. Several days later, I received a call from the police in Fairfax, Virginia. They notified me that my car was found in Fairfax parked along the highway. That is twenty to twenty-five miles from my office and to this day I haven't the slightest idea as to how it got there. Was it stolen and abandoned? Did I drive there and decide I shouldn't be driving, park it, and return to my office? If so, how did I return? In my confusion, I began to think that perhaps I drove toward Frances and Harold, the two who had befriended me years ago, and then changed my mind because of embarrassment. Your guess would be as good as mine, because this touches on a blackout about an unexplained episode.

Another episode occurred while I was in my office, under the influence of sedatives; Someone broke into my outer office and into a filing cabinet which was in the adjoining office while I was asleep in my office. Were they after drugs or money, or were they interested in the chart of a patient of mine? The patient's father worked with President Nixon. This event took place at the time of the Watergate break-in.

We say in AA that each drinking episode is worse than the previous one, and the same is often true about drugs. This episode, though of short duration, was very severe and set me back a great deal. Here is something I wrote at that time:

Why the continued suffering?
What is God's plan for me?
Could it be that he has forgotten me
or might he just be tuning me
for better things?
How gladly I would settle, not
for happiness, but the absence of pain.
Now it is the dawn and once again
I believe that all will be well.

This was written at 12:05 a.m. on November 14, 1972, during a severe depression. During this episode, I suffered a great deal of remorse, since I felt that I could blame only myself for having drifted away from Alcoholics Anonymous.

REMORSE

A few weeks later, as a result of the drugs, I entered Washington Hospital Center for 16 days. I don't remember the circumstances relating to my going to the Washington Hospital Center which was located next to the VA Hospital where I worked for years. Dr. Cresswell indicated that I was not in very good condition when I came to the emergency room. During my stay, Jim W., the first patient I had when I opened my office, visited me, and I remember his saying, "Dr. Hennigan, stop crucifying yourself - you have as much right to be sick as anyone else."

I was depressed while there, and very angry with myself, because by this time I should have known that to drift away from AA was almost certain to lead to difficulty.

Dr. Cresswell advised that I go to Willingway Hospital in Georgia, and I followed his advice. I felt it would be a bit dangerous for me to drive there by myself, dangerous because I would be more likely to use drugs if alone. So, I asked my brother-in-law to accompany me. We left

Silver Spring on December 14, 1972, stayed somewhere in South Carolina that night, and the following day drove to Statesboro, Georgia, and Willingway Hospital. Before getting out of the car, I was taking a few pills -- equanil -- when a I heard a loud voice: "What are you doing?" It was the voice of Louie from Willingway, someone who would later become a good friend. I am happy to say that those pills were the last mood-altering drugs I ever took. The date was Friday, December 15, 1972.

By the time I arrived at Willingway, I was essentially over my depression, and, although I was annoyed at myself for letting this episode happen, I knew it was not going to happen again.

Willingway was beautifully run by the late Dr. John Mooney and his wife Dot. Both were very kind, sincere, and wonderful people. We had a very nice program there -- talks by Dr. John and Dot, tapes, movies, and, several times a week, we went to AA meetings in the community. One of the patients there was an expert bridge player who told of having won a tournament which he didn't remember being in.

There was a place where most of us gathered when we weren't active with something; a place where music was usually being played. While my taste runs to Mozart and Beethoven, that was not the type of music usually played. I did accept the country music, but I suggested that it would be advisable to omit the one song "Born to Lose." They agreed with me on that suggestion.

There was one policy at the hospital which, at first, I didn't appreciate, but later realized was sensible. While there, we were not allowed to have visitors, or receive or make phone calls. It gave us a month to be free from the well-meaning but usually poor advice offered by families and friends; it also provided us with a month to focus on our sickness and concentrate on getting well.

To bring the story of my time there into perspective, and to show the different stages of the disease -- in my case, twin diseases of alcoholism and drug addiction -- I can compare two New Years' Eves: in 1952 I became drunk for the first time and had my first blackout. In 1972 I was at a party in Statesboro and was dancing with the mother-in-law of a well-known governor. From my first time of drunkenness, that is the first by my standards, to my last hospitalization, twenty years had elapsed. The fact that I mention "by my standards" is important, because my memory of the drinking episodes may be distorted because of blackouts, and because I was viewing my drinking from a false frame of reference. While I remember December 31, 1952, as the date of my first being drunk, those who knew me earlier may remember me as having been intoxicated (by normal standards) on other occasions. The alcoholic sees his drinking from his own, usually distorted, perspective. This also manifests itself in the way an alcoholic buys alcohol for a party. A friend of mine, Bob, who is in AA, told me of the time he was involved in arrangements for a picnic, and was in charge of buying the beer. He bought enough to have one case of beer per person. I remember a similar circumstance that occurred in 1957. A friend and I were having a party at her home and I was to buy the liquor. I averaged a fifth of liquor per person. You can see that the alcoholic's concept of how much people drink is clouded by his own relationship to alcohol. One of the most surprising things to me when I became sober was my realization of how little most people actually drink.

Louie, the person who first greeted me upon my arrival at Willingway, told the story of a friend of his who died as a result of alcoholism. When Louie asked the family why they hadn't considered getting him to AA, they said, "He wasn't that sick."

I remember my stay at Willingway with great pleasure. I met many wonderful people among the patients and staff, and had my first experience of being in the South, other than passing through. It was an important time in my life.

In late January 1973, I returned to Silver Spring and upon the advice of Dr. Cresswell, discontinued my practice. Being very familiar with my track record, he thought that I should take a sabbatical from psychiatry and advised that I not work for six months. I believe this was very sound advice. I lived on my retirement, really enjoyed myself, and didn't work for over a year. This was my first real break in years and I needed it.

FRUSTRATIONS WITH PSYCHOANALYSTS

Before I relate what happened in my life after Willingway, I must deal with a very unpleasant matter about which I have had many mixed feelings even to the present. I am referring to my 16 years of psychotherapy with two different psychoanalysts.

In 1957, when in desperation I felt I needed professional help, I considered what was then the "in" thing -- psychoanalysis. I made an appointment with, and saw, a well-known psychoanalyst on a Sunday morning. Despite my appearance, all the information given him about my drinking episodes and severe depression, alcoholism was never mentioned. He referred me to a colleague, whom I shall call Dr. Jones, who saw me in individual psychotherapy twice weekly at first, and then three times weekly for about six years. It was he who, when I asked for a prescription for a sedative, said, "Why don't you write your own, you're a doctor!" I cannot fault him for that, because at that time, practically any doctor would see nothing wrong with an alcoholic using sedatives.

Typically, after a session of drinking, I would go over with him the scenario as to what I had been doing, thinking, feeling, and what was going on in my life, in order to determine why I drank on this particular occasion. While all of the things we discussed about my parents, siblings, and others, may have been relevant to my emotional problems, they had nothing to do with my alcoholism and were in no way helping me in terms of my main problem. Treatment ended when it became apparent that nothing very fruitful was going to happen, and so it was arranged that I change therapists. On the last day I saw him, I asked him if he thought I was an alcoholic, and he said, "Yes, I always felt you were." Here we have a situation in which a doctor knew a patient had a fatal illness for six years, but never mentioned it to the patient.

Let us consider for a moment the course of my illness and how it could have been different if my first psychoanalyst back in 1957 had understood alcoholism. His failure to confront me about my alcoholism then led to my starting to use sedatives and tranquilizers, and eventually becoming addicted to them. My three long hospitalizations in 1968, 1969, and 1972 were all drug-related, as I had been free from alcohol since April 11, 1967. My hospitalization in 1969 led to my premature retirement from the federal government, and I was unemployed for eighteen months after my hospitalization in 1972.

Had I been properly confronted in 1957 about my alcoholism and advised to join AA as part of the condition of psychotherapy, I would have done so. Since my illness was much less severe in 1957 than it was when I joined AA in 1963, we can assume with reasonable certainty that I would have stopped drinking in 1961 or earlier, and I never would have become involved with drugs. I would have gained back eleven years of my life between 1961 and 1972, which were lost and which were an added hell for me -- all this because of an oversight, miscalculation, ignorance, or lack of knowledge on the part of a physician. This was of tremendous cost to me in terms of lost salary, missed promotions, and money spent on treatment, alcohol and drugs. What it cost in terms of damage to my body and effect on my life span, as well as my personal relationships, can only be guessed. In spite of all this, I find it difficult to be angry with this doctor, because he is a good, kind, sincere human being. He just didn't know any better.

My second analyst, whom I'll call Dr. Smith, began treating me in 1963 and continued for about 10 years. More things happened during this phase of treatment which I find less easy to forgive, but I'll tell you of my experiences and let you come to your own conclusions. I mentioned earlier that I wanted to believe that the doctors at whose hands I suffered so needlessly were not malicious, but just ill-informed. Rather than making judgments of them, I will relate the relevant events in the hope that other physicians and psychotherapists will learn from this summary of my story.

In 1963, as a result of my friend telling me he heard rumors about my being fired, I joined AA. About the same time, I changed therapists. That same year, I was hospitalized at Georgetown because of an acute anxiety reaction. I was there five days. In 1964, I was hospitalized there again as a result of an overdose of placidyl. I was there six days. The following year I was admitted there again with hematuria and was told I had a collagen disease, a fatal illness. I was there five days. Before that, I had had another hospitalization at Kalorama because of alcoholism and was there five days. In 1968 and 1969 I had several stays, including a lengthy one of six weeks, at Melwood Farm and Mar Salle. I would like the reader to guess how many times I was visited by my psychoanalyst during all of these hospitalizations between 1963 and 1969. During all that time, I was not visited by my psychoanalyst even once. Surprised? How do you think I felt, as, during each of these hospitalizations, I was severely depressed, felt totally alone in the world, and that my doctor had abandoned me? During my last hospitalization at the Washington Hospital Center in 1972, my doctor visited me once, and I believe it was only because I had finally expressed my anger about his not visiting when I had been hospitalized before.

I was hospitalized each time except for the third one in Georgetown for reasons related to alcohol or drugs; one other time I was hospitalized for an anxiety reaction. Just what did they think they were treating me for? For a doctor to abandon a severely emotionally disturbed patient, as obviously I was, is beyond my comprehension, both as a patient and a doctor. There was a time I was so depressed I even called a suicide prevention number and also made calls to a church organization; but once, when I called my second doctor, he informed me, the next time I saw him, that it was "pretty shitty" of me to call him. I had always been very conscious of not calling him, and if I did, it was only an extreme emergency. Only one time did I call at an unreasonable hour. This reminds me of the saying of Harry S. Truman, "If you can't stand the heat, get out of the kitchen." If he couldn't deal with my problems, he should have so stated and referred me elsewhere.

At one time, the subject of having a consultant see me, someone who was very knowledgeable about drugs and alcohol was discussed. Dr. Joe C. and Dr. Tony Zapalla, both of whom were well-qualified experts about alcoholism, were mentioned. I chose to see neither because I felt I knew both too well, and it would be embarrassing to me. Why wasn't this pursued? There were others who were well qualified. Either of the two I just mentioned would gladly have supplied other names.

There was another unpleasant incident involved with treatment. This was about 1972 and the beginning of 1973 when fortunately therapy ended. In order to understand this, you must know that I was severely phobic about many aspects of my life involving paperwork. Sometimes I would be very late in sending bills to my insurance company. I paid my analyst promptly at the end of each month. However, I was so disorganized and phobic I couldn't manage to send my bills to the insurance company regularly and would only manage to do so every few years. There came a time when the insurance company wouldn't pay unless the bills were sent within the year. When I finally got around to sending my bills in the last time, this could have meant my bills for 1972, 1971, and perhaps even 1970.

Because of my overall disorganization, I couldn't find all my bills, and I asked my doctor to write another set of bills for me. He did, and for this very small task charged me four hours of time. There is no way this should take more than a few minutes. I said nothing because I had just returned from Georgia, knowing that the therapy was about to end. The truth of the matter is, knowing how paralyzed I was in the matter, a way to help me should have been instituted, and it would have been no problem for him to help me fill out a form in his office or for him to do it. This cost me about $2,000 because of the lapse of time.

The last chapter regarding that relationship had to do with my decision to return to work and my getting a license to practice in Maryland. I did what was necessary to get my license, and, probably because of my medical record, was called to Baltimore to the State Medical Society for an interview. I was turned down that month. The reason? They had not yet received a letter from my analyst. He was given over a month in which to write the letter. After having me as a patient for 10 years, he couldn't even do that in a professional way.

I finally finished with psychotherapy in early 1973, and from that time on my life has improved steadily. Years ago my very dear friend, Dr. Ray Hayes, had suggested I discontinue it and I wish I had followed his advice. Let me say that to attempt to treat alcoholism with psychotherapy, that is, attempting to find a cause or find out why the alcoholic drinks on each occasion not only does no good, but it does tremendous harm. It creates the illusion that something is being done, when in reality nothing is being done. Using psychoanalytic techniques for addictions is like treating pneumonia with insulin or treating diabetes with penicillin. Psychoanalysis may have a place but it is not in treating alcoholism or drug addiction.

The search for why did I drink on each occasion eventually led me to the realization that. . .

- *I drank when I got a promotion, but I drank when I didn't get the promotion;*
- *I drank when I was depressed and I drank on the rare occasion when I was happy;*
- *I drank because I was lonely, but I drank when I was with someone;*

The reasons are as numerous as the number of alcoholics times 100. I eventually came to the very simple conclusion that an alcoholic, regardless of the reason he gives, drinks for only one reason. He drinks because he is a drug addict and alcohol is his drug.

If you, the reader, are in therapy and your therapist is trying to find out why you drink or why you became an alcoholic, run, don't walk, to the nearest exit. I do not mean to imply that no alcoholic needs psychotherapy; about 10 to 15 percent do; but the main goal of the therapist should be to get the alcoholic to AA. To try to treat symptoms without AA involvement is futile.

6. MY NEW LIFE

"My crown is in my heart, not on my head;
Not decked with diamonds and Indian stones,
Nor to be seen: my crown is called content;
A crown it is that seldom kings enjoy."
— King Henry VI, Shakespeare

Early 1973 represents the beginning of a new phase in my life. Now my life was characterized by my having finally conquered alcoholism and drug addiction. I've been alcohol-free since 1967 and drug-free since 1972. Also, I had discovered that what we call serenity in AA was available to me.

I was now living on a modest retirement from the federal government and was again living with my sister, Helen, and her family. While trying to make decisions regarding how to use my time, one thing was clear: I had to become involved in some kind of physical activity for reasons of health, for weight reduction and for moderate hypertension.

While walking on Connecticut Avenue in downtown Washington, I went into a vegetarian restaurant called the Golden Temple. It was run by a group who adopted the Sikh religion, the 3H organization. The 3H represented Health, Happy, and Holy. I talked with one of them and asked if they taught yoga, and he informed me they had classes every morning. The following day, April 25, 1973, I went to their ashram at 1704 Q Street and had my first lesson in Kundalini yoga. Before we started our lesson, we were asked to send a prayer to someone in our life, and I forced myself to pray for my former supervisor at the VA, the one I had wanted to flatten into part of the freeway with the help of the Mafia!

At the end of my first lesson, I felt more peace than I had ever known in my life. I was then age 51. Thus I realized why we spend so much time in AA talking about forgiveness and giving up our resentment and anger -- not because of what anger does to others but because of what it does to ourselves.

When I finished my first lesson in yoga, I remember saying to myself, "Leo, don't screw it up as you did AA by analyzing, questioning, and doubting; just do as they say and judge only by results." I found these people to be very positive, very gentle, very accepting, and in no way trying to convert others to their way of thinking. I have had contact with them over the years; in fact, about six years ago, I went to New Mexico and spent some time with them doing yoga and meditating.

During these first months, I heard various people who were doing yoga talk about meditation. I had heard the word meditation often but had no concept as to what it was. However, I did notice that those who spoke of meditating seemed to have a serenity which I found very desirable. Sometime in the same year, I went to a talk on transcendental meditation (T.M.) and the following weekend took the course on T.M. I was taught to meditate by Mary Belcher; and with meditation I experienced another major breakthrough. I was getting in touch with calmness and serenity in a way I had never known before. It was becoming apparent to me that my life literally had been one of constant anxiety, varying only in intensity.

Up to that time, my approach to life had been strictly western. I assumed that one would be looked upon with suspicion were one to show any interest in eastern matters such as yoga and meditation, to say nothing of more occult disciplines. However, because I had much time on my hands, great curiosity, and because it was a time of numerous movements in Washington, I looked into everything I could. I tried to look at every new experience as pleasant, as something new, and not necessarily something to be analyzed and dissected as in a laboratory. With this attitude, I found many new ideas which I've incorporated into my way of life. I have been a dabbler in most of the things I've looked into, but aware, too, that these areas attract a high percentage of charlatans.

During subsequent years, I touched base with Hatha yoga, Lifespring, loving relations, EST, rebirthing, flotation tanks, theosophy, massage workshops, seances, and lectures from diverse groups of people talking on everything from acupuncture to Zen Buddhism.

I experienced the spiritual value of eastern approaches which contrasted with much of western psychology. I viewed western psychology as basically intellectual with no concern for the spiritual part of the patient. This was a time of trying to get my life in order, alcohol and drug-free. I had mixed feelings as to whether or not I would succeed this time. I had improved my condition from the 1969 to 1972 period, when I did have a relapse, but I was afraid a relapse could happen again.

Sometime at the end of 1973, I decided to return to work and began working in various clinics in Prince George's County and one in Washington, D.C. This was during a time when changes were taking place in the field of mental health and in mental hygiene clinics. There was an attitude of "Everyone is equally qualified, regardless of experience," and I found not only a total lack of structure, but such open hostility to psychiatrists that I left various clinics. There was also the fact that, in spite of the number of patients who were alcoholics or drug addicts, there was tremendous resistance on the part of most staffs to learn about these matters. For four years I worked in four different clinics and, in 1977, began private practice in Chevy Chase. I will comment more on my experiences in these clinics in a later chapter.

OTHER PROBLEMS

Periodically, during the telling of my story about my alcoholism and drug addiction, I have mentioned other problems which seriously hampered my living successfully. There are two I would like to discuss now:

1. A fear of writing; and
2. a paralyzing phobia about anything related to paperwork.

When you consider the amount of material a physician receives and the correspondence required, you may appreciate the enormity of the writing and paperwork problems. Let us first consider my problem concerned with writing.

I graduated from medical school in 1950. My fear of writing was so great that I never wrote an article until 1980. I was so phobic that, if I were offered a large sum of money to write on any subject, I'm sure my answer would have been an emphatic "No!" It is interesting to me how eventually I managed to change.

In 1980, Maryland was to be the host state for the annual meeting of the International Doctors of Alcoholics Anonymous (I.D.A.A.), and the meetings were to be held in Baltimore. It was deemed advisable that most of the articles to appear in the October 1980 issue of the *Medical Journal of the State of Maryland* be written by doctors who were recovered alcoholics. When the subject of AA was mentioned, I offered to write an article on it, and did so.

After the meeting adjourned, I discussed with Dr. Maxwell Weisman a theory I had concerning my belief that most alcoholics remembered their first drink and could discuss it with great feeling. It was my theory that if it could be demonstrated that alcoholics did have a better memory for their first drink and recalled the drink's having a more pleasant effect than did nonalcoholics, such a fact could be used diagnostically. Such a pleasant first-drink memory could help in the early diagnosis of alcoholism. He agreed that the idea had merit and suggested I study it and write about it. I interviewed 50 alcoholics, 25 men and 25 women, and 50 nonalcoholics, also 25 men and 25 women. I simply asked them to tell me all they remembered about their first drink, and the results were quite impressive. The results demonstrated that using this question can be a very effective tool in establishing the diagnosis of alcoholism at an early stage.

I wrote an article on this study, and excerpts from it appeared in USA Today, Psychology Today, and Mademoiselle. As a result of this study, I was interviewed by various radio stations, and one, a station in Tulsa, Oklahoma, was particularly interesting. We had arranged for a telephone interview at a certain time, but unknown to me, they had four people in the radio audience standing by to be interviewed. I did interview the four of them, starting each interview by asking them to tell me all they remembered about their first drink. I was able to establish that two were alcoholics, and one of them called back to confirm this fact.

During the next few years, I began thinking about writing a book, but had so much selfdoubt that I considered writing it with a coauthor. Later, I moved from thinking about having a co-author to having a ghost writer, and having it be one of the "as told to" type of books in which the information is given to a professional writer who then writes the book. Mrs. Mary Taylor, a close friend and advisor for many years, kept encouraging me to write it myself; to believe that I could do it. I finally decided that, yes, I could do it, so this book is my third attempt at writing something. A suggestion from Mary helped me resolve my problem concerning how to proceed. One day, I was discussing my ideas regarding the early diagnosis of alcoholism, when she said, "Leo, why don't you write your book just as you are telling me about your ideas regarding alcoholism?" That was the suggestion and encouragement I needed, and I have proceeded to write in that fashion.

The other problem, the fear of paperwork, can best be described as a monster. I had trouble with everything from opening mail to dealing with income tax. Papers were piled up. More than once I have said, half-jokingly but with some sincerity, I would like to start an organization called P.R.A., Pack Rats Anonymous; there are many of us living with piles of papers, but we don't talk about it.

One of the steps of overcoming a phobia is asking oneself, "Why was I ever so afraid?" Actually, I had some brief periods of professional help which were of tremendous value in breaking through these fears. I struggled with them for years, particularly the one regarding paperwork, and made only a slight improvement on my own. Why didn't I seek professional help sooner? There were two reasons: first, I really believed I would eventually get organized and get my life in order; and second, my experiences with psychotherapy had been so bad that I had developed a very negative feeling about professional help.

I once had a part-time secretary, Becky Gatwood, who did a fine job of helping me with my difficulty about paper and with my utter disorganization. Unfortunately, she had to leave for a fulltime job, but she had started me in the right direction. Finally, despairing of bringing order into my life, I decided to try hypnosis. I asked my brotherinlaw for the name of someone who could help me, and he referred me to Dr. Nolen Bailey, a psychologist with a good reputation in the area of hypnosis. I saw him a number of times in 1983, and that also led to a major breakthrough. Soon after that I started making changes in my life. I also consulted with Mr. Jonathan Crook, and received valuable help from him. He advised me to hire another secretary, which I did, and she, Noreen O'Meara Shanbacker, has been very helpful in getting me organized.

At present, my life is the best it has ever been, and I am looking forward to becoming more involved in public speaking and to having wider opportunities to discuss alcoholism. You have accompanied me on a trip through my alcoholism and drug addiction and my ultimate recovery from these illnesses. From my first drink in January 1946 to my last drug usage on December 15, 1972, this journey, much of it through hell, took nearly 27 years.

The house on Henderson Street where I was born, 10/2/21. *Breeze Photos, Taylor Penn.*

Old Forge High School, 1935-1939 *courtesy of Sandy Furey*

St. Thomas College, 1939-1943 *courtesy of Paul S. Brown*

University of Scranton *courtesy of Paul S. Brown*

Benjamin Rush, signer of the Declaration of Independence and father of American psychiatry who first stated that alcoholism is a disease. *courtesy of the Naval Medical Archives*

Georgetown Medical School, Washington D.C. *Mike Clem, Georgetown Educational Media*

St. Elizabeths Hospital, Washington D.C. where I was an intern from 1950-1952 and where my alcoholism first became apparent.

2001 Kalaroma Street, Washington D.C., 1963 *photo by Mike Clem*

Restaurant where I had my first drink at age 24 *Breeze Photos, Taylor Penn.*

Mt. Carmel, Paterson N.J. *Artistic Photography*

Edgar Allen Poe, who recognized the devastating effects of this disease we call alcoholism, and wrote about it in his story "The Black Cat" (see Appendix B).

My niece, Carol Anne, and me just prior to my joining AA

PART TWO

A New Approach to Dealing Effectively With our Number One Health Problem — Alcoholism

INTRODUCTION

"There is one thing stronger than all the armies in the world, and that is an idea whose time has come."

— Victor Hugo

When I finally recovered from alcoholism and drug addiction, I experienced a whole gamut of emotions: at first, gratitude that I had finally conquered two enemies; then, surprise at the fact that I was capable of sustained happiness. I had long since given up on expecting happiness and was willing to settle for not hurting.

My next emotion was anger; or, should I say hatred, as being more appropriate to describe my feeling toward those physicians who had treated me so badly. Most of my hate was directed at a few people where I worked who were senior to me. As to the internists I had in the 1960s and the psychoanalysts, my feeling was confusion. How could they have been so inept? Why did none of them do what has always been accepted in the practice of medicine -- bring in a consultant who knew something about which they were ignorant? You have read how eventually I learned to deal with my hate-anger-bitterness, because this was an integral part of my recovery from alcoholism. Once I had dealt with these negative emotions, I became concerned about how many alcoholics suffered and died; and how many more were to be misdiagnosed, mistreated, and die because of the poor way society deals with alcoholism.

As I look back, I am amazed that so many years went by during which I felt guilty because of the ineptness of my treatment; and how long it took me to say to myself, "Damn it, I was victimized severely by the medical system, and so are many others." Eventually, as I was able to get over all the remorse, pain, bitterness, and wish for revenge, I asked myself, "What are you going to do about dealing with alcoholism in America?"

I finally decided to take a long, hard look at this disease, and, having done so, develop some new concepts; I am now in a position to do something, that is, write this book. Just as I asked you to join me on a journey through my alcoholism, I am going to ask you to join me on another journey; that is, investigating why alcoholism remains such a problem in our society.

It has been said that it may be normal to act abnormally under abnormal conditions. Alcoholism is not treated as a typical disease and is not approached in a normal manner. It should be.

One of the reasons alcoholism has remained such a problem, I feel, is that it has never really been looked at in the proper perspective. Let's do that now.

1. WHAT IS ALCOHOLISM

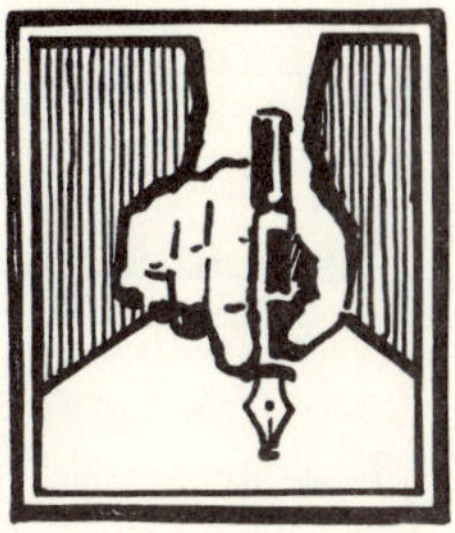

"If a fatal disease were to invade our country, affect six million Americans, adversely affect the lives of 24 million others, cost our economy 25 billion dollars a year, we might consider declaring a national emergency. Such a disease is upon us -- it is called alcoholism."

— Dr. Ruth Fox

Many people feel that alcoholism is not a disease, but a weakness or a condition which is self-imposed. For myself, I am satisfied with the idea that, "If it kills you and it's not an accident, it must be a disease;" but I understand that this reason is not enough for most people. Therefore, let us examine some other options.

Benjamin Rush, father of American psychiatry, signer of the Declaration of Independence, and Surgeon General under George Washington, stated that it was a disease. In Rush's *Medical Inquiries and Observations Upon the Diseases of the Mind* (1830 edition), he stated that, "the use of strong drink is at first the effect of free agency. From habit it takes place from necessity." Then he adds, ". . . persons . . . devoted to the use of ardent spirits (are) irreclaimable. . . ." (Appendix A). I find it both interesting and tragic that Benjamin Rush in the eighteenth century and in the nineteenth century Edgar Allan Poe, an alcoholic and author of *The Black Cat* (Appendix B), knew that alcoholism was a disease, but tragically many doctors today still don't know this.

It is difficult to treat an illness effectively when it is seen as a sin or a weakness. In the 1952 *Diagnostic and Statistical Manual* (DSM, I) of the American Psychiatric Association, alcoholism was classified under "Sociopathic Personality Disturbance." The description of alcoholics and those in this category was of "individuals ill primarily in terms of society. . . ." (Appendix C).

In 1968 the *Diagnostic and Statistical Manual of Mental Disorders* (DSM, II) of the American Psychiatric Association, alcoholism -- classified under "Personality Disorders" -- was included in the description: "This group of disorders is characterized by deeply ingrained maladaptive patterns of behavior. . . ." (Appendix D). Alcoholism, here and also in the above-mentioned example, was listed under the category which included "Sexual Deviations."

The 1980 DSM, III, classification for alcoholism was under both

. . . .

1987 DSM, IIIR (revised), the following were listings for alcoholism: "Psychoactive Use Disorders" and "Psychoactive Substance-Induced Organic Mental Disorders."

Let us look at some other definitions of the alcoholic. The first, tinged with a little ironic humor, comes from one of my former professors in medical school, Dr. Isadore Rodis. He said, "An alcoholic is a person who can take it or leave it but always takes it." Another colleague said, "An alcoholic is a person who spends most of his time thinking about drinking or thinking about not drinking."

Some medical definitions of alcoholism include:

> *"The extreme dependence on excessive amounts of alcohol, associated with a cumulative pattern of deviant behavior."*
>
> — Nurses Reference Library

> *"A chronic behavioral disorder manifested by repeated drinking of alcoholic beverages in excess of the dietary and social uses of the community and to an extent that interferes with the drinker's health or his social or economic functioning; some degree of habituation, dependence, or addiction is implied.*
>
> — Dorland's Medical Dictionary, 26th edition

> *"Alcohol abuse may be suspected when an individual shows evidence of a psychologic dependence on alcohol or a need for alcohol to continue daily functioning."*
>
> —American Psychiatric Association

> *"Alcoholism is a chronic illness characterized by a physical and mental dependence on alcoholic beverages. Such dependence has severely detrimental effects on physical, emotional, and economic well being, which may combine to shorten the alcoholic's life span by 10-12 years."*
>
> — Professional Guide to Diseases, 1982

The World Health Organization (WHO) has defined "alcohol-type drug dependence" as existing . . . *"when the consumption of alcohol exceeds the limits that are accepted by his culture; if an individual consumes alcohol at times that are deemed inappropriate . . . intake of alcohol becomes so great as to injure his health or impair his social relationships."*

I believe alcoholism is a chronic progressive disease characterized by a love for alcohol which leads to abnormal drinking. This ultimately leads to problems in the area of health, family, work, and society. I emphasize the word "ultimately" to make it clear that alcoholism may exist for years without presenting problems.

I ask the reader to note that most of these definitions tend to give the impression that alcoholism is diagnosable only when health or social relationships are impaired.

It is my contention that we have focused much too long on diagnosing alcoholism in its advanced stages and have ignored what has always been emphasized in the practice of medicine, **early diagnosis.**

Two of the most significant signs of alcoholism are the two which occur early in the disease, and their presence should lead us in the direction of making the diagnosis of alcoholism:

- Occasional relief drinking, and
- Increased tolerance (more and more drinks).

You will note, in my description of my drinking, that I was an alcoholic from the onset of my drinking; but it was years before my social relationships and health were affected.

In my opinion, no disease can approach alcoholism in the amount of pain, anguish, and suffering it causes. Because of the prejudicial attitudes we have about alcoholism, we often fail to focus on the total impact it has on our society. It is my contention that it is a rare American who, during the course of his life, doesn't suffer from the effects of alcoholism, either his own or that of someone else's. Our tendency is to feel that until it happens to us, or to someone close to us, we tend to ignore it, much as we do with crimes of violence; ignore them until one strikes close to home.

Let us look at some basic statistics about this disease and then look at some specific examples of the devastating effects of alcoholism; or, in some cases where alcoholism is not certain, on the impact caused by the injudicious use of alcohol.

In Dennis Wholey's book *The Courage to Change*, G. Douglas Talbott, M.D., makes some very pertinent comments about alcoholism, some of which I recently discussed with him. Dr. Talbott is responsible for one of the best programs in the country for helping the impaired physician. He feels that the old figures of 10 million alcoholics in America and one drinker in ten becoming an alcoholic are obsolete. His opinion is that one in seven who drink become alcoholics, and that we probably have 22 million alcoholics in this country. It is usually accepted that each alcoholic adversely affects the life of four others, so we have untold numbers of Americans affected by alcoholism.

The National Council on Alcoholism estimates that alcoholics have 58 times the suicide rate of nonalcoholics. (*Medical Tribune*, Wednesday, June 19, 1985). The National Institute of Alcohol Abuse and Alcoholism (NIAAA) in 1975 estimated that 11 percent of all deaths are alcohol-related (*Canadian Medical Journal*, May 1981). According to *Alcoholism Today: The Progress and the Promise* by Carol Hegarty (Compcare, 1983):

80% of fire deaths are alcohol-related;

65% of drownings are alcohol-related;

22% of home accidents are alcohol-related;

77% of falls are alcohol-related;

36% of accidents to pedestrians are alcohol-related;

55% of arrests are alcohol-related;

25-33% of suicides and homicides are alcohol-related;

30% of divorce and juvenile delinquency cases are associated with alcoholism in a family member;

90% of reported child abuse cases implicate alcohol;

there is a positive relationship between alcoholic drinking and ulcers, diabetes, and heart disease.

According to the Illinois Action on Alcoholic Problems, alcoholism is the number one cause of death among persons aged 15-24. In 1976, there were 46,081 deaths among this age group. The causes of death were:

1. accidents;
2. murder;
3. suicide;
4. cancer and;
5. heart disease.

"The truth of the matter is alcohol caused most of the accidents, murders, and one-third of the suicides."

— Illinois Action on Alcoholic Problems

The Washington State Council on Alcoholism, an affiliiate of the National Council on Alcoholism, estimates the following:

- *50% of juvenile delinquents have family members with a drinking problem.*

- *A correlation exists between battered wives, child neglect, child abuse, and alcohol use.*

- *The heavy use of alcohol by women during pregnancy may result in abnormalities in the child, termed fetal alcohol syndrome.*

- *Still-births and miscarriages are of a high frequency among women who drink heavily during pregnancy.*

- *9 of 10 husbands leave the alcoholic wife.*

- *9 of 10 wives stay with the alcoholic husband.*

On May 5, 1985, the Washington Post cited alcohol as a killer in Washington, D.C. More than half the recent deaths were linked to drink. The report mentioned:

- *three-fifths of homicides were related to drinking;*
- *38% of suicides were related to drinking;*
- *one-half of highway deaths were related to drinking;*
- *43% of firearm deaths were related to drinking;*
- *77% of cutting and stabbing deaths were related to drinking;*
- *64% of blunt force deaths were related to drinking;*
- *47% of deaths by falls were related to drinking;*
- *86% of deaths from exposure were related to drinking;*
- *43% of pedestrian deaths were related to drinking;*

The article also cites an incident of two children who died from burns and could have been saved if the father had not been drunk.

These have been some basic facts. Now I would like to present some specific examples (many are news items) to demonstrate why alcoholism is our number one health problem:

> *Miami Dolphins running back* ***David Overstreet*** *was legally intoxicated when he died in a high-speed crash near his east Texas hometown last month.*
>
> — Washington Post, July 5, 1984

> ***Gig Young,*** *wife found slain in New York. . . It would appear that he shot her and then shot himself. Friends said that Young had developed skin cancer and was plagued throughout his adult life by a drinking problem.*
>
> — Washington Post

> ***Dylan Thomas*** *was one of the finest poets of our time. . . . One alcoholic binge too many proved fatal; he died at St. Vincent's Hospital on November 9, 1953, after lying four and one-half days in a coma. He was 39.*
>
> — The New York Times, July 7, 1985

One of the most tragic stories I know describes a young woman who was twice the victim of alcohol-related accidents. The second time she died. In 1972, Gail Tietjen was given up for dead when the police found her two hours after her date had wrecked his sports car while driving under the influence of alcohol. When she awakened from a coma several days later, she did not know her family, she did not know herself. She struggled for seven years to regain some semblance of normalcy. Her life ended when her small car was hit head on by a wrong way driver on highway 85 in Cupertino, California. Ninety minutes later she was dead. She was 25. The driver of the other car, who walked away from the crash, was a 59-year-old who was charged with driving under the influence.

> ***John Bonham*** *of the Led Zeppelin died in September 1980 from choking after a drinking binge. He was 32.*

> ***Dennis Wilson*** *of the Beach Boys drowned in December 1983 after drinking. He was 42.*

> ***Kris Kristofferson*** *says he got a jolt seeing himself playing scenes he couldn't remember because he was so "bombed."*

A recent study of the rail workforce concluded that 20 percent of employees are drunk when they arrive at work or get drunk there at least once a year, compared with 1.5 percent of adult males in the national workforce. Although only 18 to 19 percent of American males in general get drunk at least once a year, about 150,000 of the 234,000 rail workers got drunk at least once yearly. In 1978, there were 174,000 violations of the rule against drinking while on the job or while subject to call, but only 900 were reported and investigated. The study showed drinking appeared to be heavily related to accidents, damage to properties, and injuries.

> ***THREE N. VA. MEN, THREE OTHERS KILLED IN TRAFFIC GAME.***
> *Fredericksburg, Va., October 8. Six people were killed and four others seriously injured when a pickup truck playing "a game of Russian Roulette" crossed into the left lane of a two-lane highway and smashed into a car. The driver of the truck, according to the 30-year-old survivor in the truck, had been drinking heavily as had the rest of his passengers. The injured man begged the driver to slow down but to no avail.*

> ***A TEARFUL FUNERAL FOR FAMILY OF FIVE. NEW CHARGE IN ACCIDENT THAT KILLED SEVEN.***
> *Robert L. Williams, 41, while on parole, was driving a car which slammed into a crowd at a bus stop and killed seven people. Among the seven were a husband and wife, both age 24, and their three children. The driver of the car had a blood level of .10 percent and was driving at 70 and 80 miles per hour. Also killed were an 18-year-old and a 6-month-old child.*
>
> — Washington Post, August 31, 1984

Several years ago, in the Washington, D.C., area, 12 teenagers died in an accident. The driver of the pickup truck, also in his teens, had been drinking. Within a year, another such accident happened in Virginia, and this time five died. Alcohol was involved, reports stated. Several years ago, near Scranton, Pa., eight teenagers died in an automobile accident. Alcohol was involved, reports again stated.

In the five accidents noted above, 38 people died, most of them teenagers, children, or young adults. What a tragedy! What a waste! Are you beginning to see why alcoholism is our number one health problem? Are you beginning to see that it is everyone's business?

"Dear Abby," a syndicated news column, printed a powerful message called "Please God, I'm only 17." In the column she tells of a 17-year-old driving too fast, then death, and after death, his thoughts as she imagined them. He reviews the crash, being placed in a drawer, his family identifying him, the funeral. He says, "Wake me up! Please don't bury me! Please God, I'm only 17." What a powerful message it is.

I have attempted, without boring you with too many statistics, to demonstrate that alcoholism is our number one health problem. Just stop for a moment, close this book, and think of the 38 who died in five accidents. Is there any way we can measure the suffering of the families, friends, and neighbors -- just from these 38 deaths?

Think of several teenagers you know, maybe in your own family, or next door neighbors. Can you imagine the suffering if even one were to die tragically in an accident?

Yes, there is absolutely no doubt in my mind but that alcoholism is our number one health problem. No other illness causes as much suffering to the victim and others. The most tragic thing about all of this is not so much the number of deaths, but that it is so unnecessary.

2. ALCOHOLISM: A DISEASE OF DENIAL

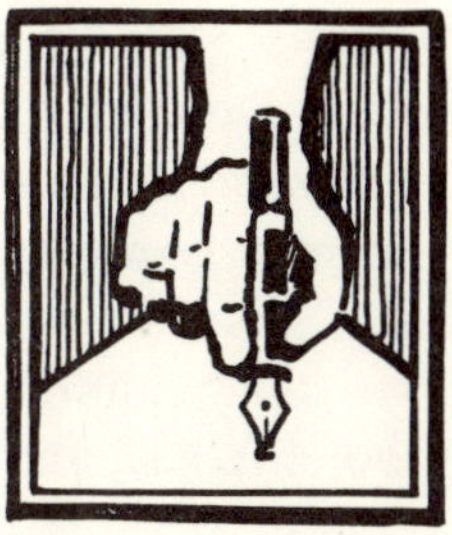

"The greatest derangement of the mind is to believe something is true because one wishes it to be so."

— Louis Pasteur

It has been said that if we want to know what our faults are, look at the faults we find in others. This is interesting because we accuse alcoholics of denying their alcoholism. Denial is one of the mechanisms we all use to maintain stability in the face of a threatening situation. The child may close her eyes or put her hand over her eyes so that a threatening object will disappear. What is our first reaction when told of the death of a loved one, or told we have a fatal disease, such as when I was told I had a collagen disease? "I don't believe it." It is particularly interesting that only the alcoholic is not allowed this means of defense, even though alcoholism carries with it all sorts of implications beyond it's merely being an illness.

We are still struggling with our prejudices about alcoholism that make the alcoholic a bad person, not a sick person. Yet we expect the alcoholic to admit he is an alcoholic. How unrealistic!

During the past month I saw two references in a local newspaper about reformed alcoholics; "reformed" is a word appropriate for criminals, but not for sick people.

Denial enables us to muster our defenses so that we can ignore unpleasant realities. Yes, alcoholism is a disease of denial, but I'm referring to the denial of physicians, psychologists, social workers, nurses, and others in the medical community. It is also denied by parents when told about their child being an alcoholic; it is denied by children when told their parent is an alcoholic; it is denied by society which finds it convenient to point to the victim, the alcoholic, and accuse him of denying his illness.

To demonstrate the malevolent role of denial, I shall give you examples. Why not start with some with which you are familiar -- the ones involving me. I won't even mention the several hundred professionals with whom I worked during all my years, but will mention only the ones with whom I had a relationship as a patient.

In 1957, I consulted with a leading psychoanalyst who in spite of my drinking history, etc., never mentioned alcoholism. In 1960, a leading internist with whom I consulted never mentioned alcoholism. In 1963, the doctor to whom the doctor above referred me never mentioned alcoholism even though my chart showed I mentioned drinking a fifth a day. In 1964, the same doctor, having the above information and now knowing of a hospitalization at a detoxification place, never mentioned alcoholism. He also never mentioned it when I was hospitalized in 1965. The first analyst saw me six-to-seven years and mentioned alcoholism only in the last session when I asked him if I were an alcoholic.

Not one of my bosses ever discussed alcoholism with me.

Let me give you some other examples of denial:

I told an obstetrician about my specialty -- treating alcoholics -- and his response was, "I don't have any alcoholics -- I'm an obstetrician." Apparently, he had never heard of the fetal alcohol syndrome.

A pediatrician told me he didn't need to know about alcoholism as all his patients were children. When I asked him if he had treated battered children and children with serious emotional problems, he said, "Yes." And I said, "You don't think there's a relationship between these conditions and the drinking habits of the parents?"

Children do become alcoholics at an early age, as one woman I interviewed, when I did a study in 1980, remembers drinking at age four-and-a-half and liking it, and having her first blackout at age 10

An orthopedic surgeon, at a seminar on alcoholism, questioned his need to know about alcoholism. I asked if he didn't treat many accident victims, and he said he did. I then suggested that maybe many of the broken bones which he set were alcohol-related.

A social worker told me about discussing the alcoholism of a young female patient at a state hospital in Maryland with a psychologist who said the patient's alcoholism was only secondary to her schizophrenia. You can't get more bizarre in your thinking!

I am currently treating a young psychologist whose mother called me two years ago and told me about his drinking habits and his behavior. When I said it sounds like alcoholism, her reaction was one of disbelief and denial. A year later, she called again and this time both mother and son came to see me. He had been seeing a social worker who treated his depression without even focusing on the fact that he was depressed because he was drinking a depressant -- alcohol. She completely missed his alcoholism. However, he has told me what a good therapist she was, and I said, "How can she be a good therapist when she didn't even diagnose your alcoholism?" Now the son is currently doing well in AA and in therapy.

At this point, it is necessary to comment upon the fact that we alcoholics have been brainwashed to believe it is our responsibility to make the diagnosis, not the doctor's or the therapist's.

One of my patients had previously been treated by another psychiatrist. When he came to one of his sessions under the influence, he told his psychiatrist that he drank so much coffee he couldn't sleep, so he drank alcohol to help him sleep. His psychiatrist advised him to give up coffee. As you may guess, not only was alcoholism never mentioned, but he prescribed Valium long enough to get the patient addicted to that, too.

The first day I worked in one clinic some 12 years ago, a social worker who had been treating a 16-year-old female for three months for depression had me examine the patient. Within minutes, I made the diagnosis of alcoholism and drug addiction. The patient was referred to Dr. Joe C., who had her treated at Montgomery General Hospital for detoxification, and after four weeks at Seneca, an alcohol rehabilitation center, she made a very uneventful recovery. The social worker, well meaning but obviously very naive, had said, "You don't ask a 16-year-old if they drink or use drugs."

A 13-year-old girl who had been seen by social workers and psychologists was referred to me for evaluation. She had stopped going to school, and I couldn't find the cause of her depression until I asked her to tell me about her parents' drinking. She immediately began crying and the mystery was solved. It appears her father was drinking six to eight beers a night, his behavior was unpredictable, and she was ashamed to bring her friends home. Fortunately, both parents were very understanding, and the father started attending AA and the mother Al-Anon.

Because of a change in administration, patients from another clinic were referred to the one where I was a consultant. I saw a 60-year-old woman who had been going to another clinic for years and had been on tranquilizers all those years without any change in her condition. The second time I saw her, I asked about her husband's drinking, and she began crying.

Still another patient who had been totally mistreated had her life changed when the alcoholism of her husband was diagnosed and properly treated. They both started in AA and Al-Anon, and a year later I met them at a meeting and both were celebrating a year of affiliation with AA and Al-Anon.

The cases involving the 13-year-old girl and the 60-year-old woman should make clear a basic principle in treating any patient with emotional problems. It is imperative that the physician or therapist not only take a thorough alcohol history of the patient, but also ask about the drinking habits of other family members. You may be reasonably certain that, unless specifically asked, many patients will not volunteer information about the drinking habits of family members.

In the book, *Current Therapy,* 1980 edition, an article by Marc Galanter, M.D., and Stephen H. Bender, M.D., stated that 15 to 50 percent of general medical beds in hospitals are occupied by alcoholics. While they do not specify it, the chances are that most of these patients do not have their alcoholism diagnosed, and if diagnosed, are probably not receiving treatment for this illness.

Let us take a more conservative, but no doubt factual, view and accept 25 to 35 percent. This means that every fourth or every third patient in your average hospital has a fatal disease which is seldom diagnosed and more rarely treated. I hope the reader is getting the message, particularly about the impact of denial.

3. ALCOHOLISM: A DISEASE OF APATHY

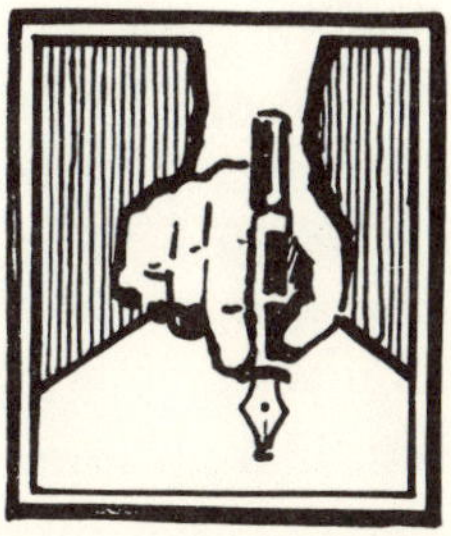

"The worst sin toward our fellow creatures is not to hate them but to be indifferent to them; that's the essence of inhumanity."
— The Devil's Disciple, George Bernard Shaw

It has long been my belief that alcoholics do not die of alcoholism -- they die of neglect. Since my recovery from alcoholism, I have attempted to help educate people about alcoholism. What has stood out more than anything else is the resistance I have encountered from physicians, psychologists, social workers, educators, members of the clergy, and others. Their choosing to hold on to their lack of knowledge is literally unbelievable.

People resist change. We know that to be true. Resisting change is especially exemplified by professionals regarding alcoholism and the alcoholic.

At the clinic where I saw the 16-year-old alcoholic and drug addict, I presided at a weekly case conference. When her case was presented to the staff, I suggested that all the staff members begin to attend AA meetings in order to become more familiar with alcoholism and drug addiction. Four weeks later, a case was presented concerning a family that had been known to the clinic. Over the years there had been many crises in the family. As the case was discussed, only one staff member even mentioned that the father was an alcoholic. They totally ignored the impact that he and his illness had on the family. During those four weeks, not one staff member had attended an AA meeting as suggested.

Of the first eleven patients I saw in that clinic, alcoholism, drug addiction, or both, were present in six of the eleven cases. Most important was the fact that not one of the staff recognized them as conditions about which something could be done. Not one of the staff recognized their need to learn about alcoholism and drug addiction.

Several years ago, I talked to a professional group which was having a seminar on burnout. I pointed out that one of the main causes of burnout among people in the field of mental health is their lack of knowledge about alcoholism, and consequently, their lack of success in treating a high percentage of their patients. Since a high percentage of patients in any clinic, or patients seen privately by those treating emotional problems, are certain to be alcoholics, it is mandatory that every therapist understand alcoholism.

My feeling was that this suggestion fell on deaf ears. During that conference on burnout, I met a minister who stated that 70 percent of the problems that came his way were alcohol-related. I offered to meet with him to teach him about alcoholism. The offer was made in June 1984, and although he lives within five miles of me, I have yet to hear from him.

A year ago, in my doctor's office, I was talking to a young priest, and he gave me the same answer when I asked him what percentage of the problems that came his way were alcohol-related. I made the same offer to him, and the results were the same -- he showed no interest in learning about an illness that represents 70 percent of the problems which come to him.

Since I am not, and have chosen not to be anonymous for years, I speak freely of my alcoholism in social situations and have many people ask me questions about alcoholism and its treatment.

To many teachers I have offered to talk to their class on alcoholism and drug addiction, but very few accept this offer. Two who invited me to talk to their classes were two Montgomery County teachers, Ms. Carol Cook and Ms. Lois Violo.

A close-to-home example of apathy involves the University of Scranton, my alma mater. Several years ago, I gave an all-day seminar on alcoholism and drug addiction at the University. The following year I gave another all-day seminar on a Friday, but this time I had arranged to have a special meeting for the faculty members at 7:00 p.m., the previous evening. It was also arranged that each faculty member receive a notice about the meeting from the University president.

Considering the nature of the meeting, alcoholism and drug addiction, and the fact that I was an alumnus of the university, how many of the 200 faculty members do you think attended? Only six! This apathy was not characteristic of the students as they manifested considerable interest.

The next incident is one with which you have some familiarity. It has to do with the tragic death of Len Bias, basketball star at the University of Maryland. Len Bias died as much from apathy as from drug addiction.

In 1979, I became a member of the Retired Volunteer Service Corps (RVSC) at the University and offered to spend one half-day per week teaching about alcoholism and drug addiction. During the six years of my involvement with the program, I:

- talked to a class of 25 students;
- appeared on one TV program with the psychologist in charge;
- met with a psychiatrist and her group therapy session of three students -- all three had experienced blackouts after drinking, but alcoholism was never mentioned by the psychiatrist;
- met with another psychiatrist with whom I spent three hours at a booth during an alcohol-awareness day.

From the beginning, I had emphasized my wish to talk to students. I suggested the University provide a room for me for this purpose and publicize this in the school newspaper. This never occurred. Had the University been using my services, it is possible that the death of Len Bias -- and others -- could have been avoided. I resigned from the program on May 2, 1985. The following letters speak for themselves. The first is a letter to the Coordinator of RVSC.

May 2, 1985

Dear Dr. ------ :

I do not enjoy writing this letter, but I feel in good conscience I must. . . . I am a psychiatrist who is concerned about the welfare of a number of students at the University of Maryland statistically, at least 4,000 who are experiencing difficulty with alcohol and drugs.

I myself have recovered from alcoholism and drug addiction, and thus have firsthand knowledge of these illnesses.

Early in 1979, I offered my services to the RVSC and became a member of your organization. At that time, and to date, I was willing to donate one half-day a week to the University of Maryland to be used at the discretion of RVSC; however, I did say that my time would be used more effectively if arrangements were made for me to talk weekly to groups of students.

Let me give you a quick run-down of what has happened.

April 9, 1979, I sat in on a group therapy session with the psychiatrist, an aclohol counselor, and three students. All three students had a history of blackouts, but no one had apparently considered alcoholism. Although I offered to talk with the staff of the clinic, this was not acted upon.

January 1982, my next contact was a call from RVSC. Again I made the same offer, that I was available to talk with students.

January 19, 1982, you called suggesting I contact a certain psychiatrist, Dr. X. On January 27, 1982, I met Dr. X.

February 9, 1982, I participated in your alcohol awareness day. I mentioned my willingness to talk with Dr. X.'s clinic staff, but was told they had recently had a lecture or two on alcoholism, and that another would be "overkill."

December 8, 1982, I appeared on a TV show with you.

January 28, 1983, you called me and suggested I call a certain psychologist, Dr. Y. I did; again expressed my availability. Again nothing happened.

October 6, 1983, I lectured to a class of yours on alcoholism and drug addiction.

January 20, 1984, was my last contact with you when you called me and mentioned another psychologist you wanted me to meet. I could not see myself embarking on what would be another wild goose chase.

Quite simply, I, a qualified authority in the field of alcoholism and drug addiction, offered the University of Maryland my time to teach your students about alcoholism and drug addiction, and nothing has come of it in over six years. You have almost 40,000 students; at least 10 percent of them need help; I offered this help and it wasn't used. . . . I am no longer to be considered a member of the RVSC.

Copies of this letter were sent to both the President and the Chancellor of the University. Neither of them acknowledged it, although they did receive it. The response from Dr. ------ follows:

May 16, 1985

Dear Leo,

I received your correspondence of May 2, and I can appreciate the frustration you feel about your attempts to provide counseling and consultation regarding alcohol and drug abuse on campus.

I, too, was frustrated by this effort. While I have been an RVSC Coordinator, there have been three different time periods when we have tried to find a suitable placement for you. The sites that we contacted were the Health Center, The Campus Mental Health Program, The Counseling Center, The Adult Health and Human Development Program and The Student Activities Program. My last attempt was in the fall semester. But I found we had come full circle -- being recommended to the people we had already approached. As you documented in your letter, we would set up appointments fully confident that an appropriate program would be worked out. Unfortunately, this was not the case. . . .

My relationship with the University of Maryland reopened with the cocaine death of Len Bias, University basketball player, in June 1986. For me, this tragedy emphasized the fact that alcoholism is a disease of apathy, as is drug addiction. If the University of Maryland had accepted my offer in 1979, Len Bias would have been offered the opportunity to learn about alcoholism and drug addiction every year that he was a student at the University. Had this been done, maybe his death would have been prevented. It is my conviction that Len Bias died as much from apathy on the part of the University of Maryland as he did from cocaine.

Up to that point, the apathy demonstrated by the University of Maryland was by far the worst. It was not the only time it happened since I made a similar offer to my alma mater, Georgetown University, an offer which was rejected. Media apathy soon overshadowed these events. I naively believed that television stations, newspapers, medical publications, and the Department of Education would want to publicize the problem of drug abuse in schools and on campuses. They did not.

I contacted representatives of three organizations who purport to be concerned about the problem of drunk driving. Not one of them showed the slightest interest in the matter. Only one local television station, WTTG, seemed cooperative. I appeared on the station's news program for about 10 seconds, long enough to mention my feelings about apathy regarding drug addiction, but my case regarding the University of Maryland was not presented.

I made other efforts to present information about apathy of the University of Maryland on the subject of substance abuse. Because of her known interest in drug abuse and her work in this field, I sent pertinent material to then First Lady Nancy Reagan, and she forwarded the material to the Department of Education. As a result, I was contacted by an official of the Department of Education and invited to the White House for a ceremony in honor of the Department's new publication on illegal drug use in the nation's schools. While the ceremony was pleasant, the Department of Education showed no interest in taking any action about the lack of substance abuse education at the University of Maryland or elsewhere. Later, I left pertinent material with the official's secretary. I asked that the official contact me regarding educational efforts on drug abuse. To date, I have not heard from him.

Even my subsequent letter to the Governor of Maryland, his letter to the University, and the president's letter to the Chancellor accomplished nothing regarding education on student substance abuse.

If we were dealing with a "respectable" illness -- one caused by an organism -- and if I asserted that an epidemic at the University of Maryland was related to a contaminated source of water, I assure you there would have been no problem in getting the attention of the University, the newspapers, television stations, and magazines.

Apathy can't be seen under a microscope, but it is real and it is present -- in the hearts of people.

4. ABNORMAL DRINKING

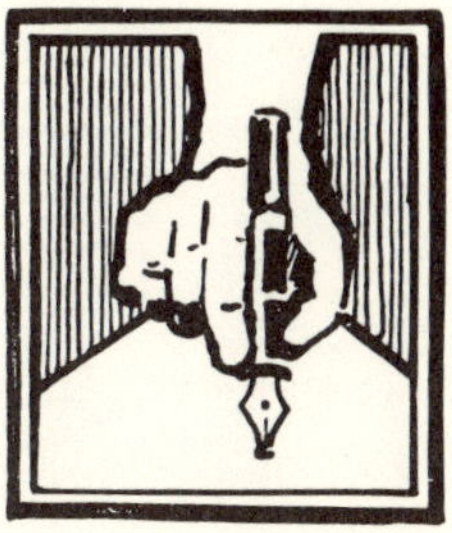

"Facts do not cease to exist because they are ignored."

— Aldous Huxley

In the field of medicine, we are always thinking of "abnormal" as compared to what is "normal." For example, a fever is considered an abnormal temperature, hypertension is an abnormal blood pressure, and tachycardia is an abnormal pulse. I believe that a lot of difficulty could be avoided if we were to think of alcoholism as "abnormal drinking."

An alcoholic who does all his drinking at home may never drink in a place that is abnormal for drinking; it may take years before an alcoholic will be involved in morning drinking.

When my drinking was at its worst, I had a custom whereby on Saturdays I often went to Gusti's at 19th and M at 11:30 a.m., had three double Manhattans, ate, bought a pint of whiskey, went to a movie and sat in the back row and drank. What could be more abnormal than this pattern?

People become defensive, in fact, angry when I say that alcoholism is abnormal drinking. I have found this even among recovered alcoholics, including doctors. When I talk about abnormal drinking, I'm immediately deluged with stories about, "My Uncle Charlie, who's been drinking heavily for 20 years, and he's not an alcoholic; I know people who drink heavily but they can stop any time they want." Recently I was told, "I know someone who has three D.W.I.s (driving while intoxicated), but he's not addicted to alcohol."

Most people will use other words to avoid saying "alcoholism." I know a very attractive young woman who is active in AA, and repeatedly doctors have tried to convince her she is not an alcoholic. They find it particularly difficult to make the diagnosis of alcoholism with a young, attractive woman. Another young, attractive woman was told by her doctor that she was a "situational alcoholic." I don't know what that means, but I see it as another example of denial on the part of the medical establishment.

The excellent book, *Alcoholism in the Professions* by LeClair Bissell, M.D., and Paul Haberman, contains some interesting quotations by doctors who are alcoholics, as follows:

> *"Relatively few subjects reported being sent by professionals to AA or to a specialized treatment facility."*
>
> *"Thirty-nine percent of physicians reported a treating person told them they weren't alcoholic."*
>
> *"When subjects claim to have told the whole truth about their drinking to a treating person, 49 percent of the men and 19 percent of the women said they still had their alcoholism specifically denied."*

The anxiety caused by the diagnosis, "alcoholism," leads to overuse of such phrases as "problem drinker," "binge drinker," and "heavy drinker." My concern is the overuse of these terms by those in the medical community, or by well-meaning friends who will choose to use these terms to avoid the term "alcoholism." In my experience, in most cases where someone was described as a heavy drinker or a problem drinker, that person, when questioned carefully, was definitely an alcoholic.

It is not uncommon to hear someone say, "My husband drinks too much, but he is not an alcoholic." "My son drinks too much, but he's not an alcoholic." The list could go on about "my girlfriend," "boyfriend," "mother," "father," etc.

This brings to mind an experience I had when I began working in a clinic. A social worker brought a patient of his to me. He said, "My patient is not an alcoholic." Why was he so defensively telling me what the patient was not? I felt certain, before I saw the patient, he was an alcoholic, and indeed, when I saw George H., it was obvious that he was.

In his book, *The Disease Concept of Alcoholism*, Dr. E. M. Jellinek describes the types of alcoholism as Alpha, Beta, Gamma, Delta, Epsilon. The reader need only know that Alpha alcoholism is often referred to as problem drinking. The predominant type of alcoholism seen in America and the one with which we are concerned is Gamma alcoholism.

Let me demonstrate our irrational fears regarding the diagnosis of alcoholism. If a doctor, upon biopsing a mass in a woman's breast, finds it to be malignant, is he doing her a favor by telling her it is benign? Were my physicians helping me by refraining from saying to me that I was an alcoholic? You have read my story and know the answer to that.

Let us imagine that a patient, John, comes to my office. Whatever his reason for consulting me, during the course of the first session, I will, of course, ask him questions as to how he uses alcohol, simply because this should be part of any examination, and because statistically the percentage of alcoholics in any group of patients is high.

Only four conclusions regarding his relationship to alcohol can be reached:

A. I diagnose him as being an alcoholic and he is an alcoholic.

B. I diagnose him as not an alcoholic and he isn't an alcoholic.

C. I diagnose him as an alcoholic when he is not an alcoholic.

D. I diagnose him as not an alcoholic when in fact he is an alcoholic.

We can obviously disregard A and B as they are correct, and direct our attention to C., the one that causes so much fear in people and for no valid reason.

First, let me ask you, the reader, how many cases do you know where someone was diagnosed as being an alcoholic when he wasn't? Let me assure you, although it could happen, it is a rare occurrence when such a misdiagnosis could adversely effect one's life. But suppose, horror of horrors, it were to happen; what is the great tragedy?

You must first know that in order for me to say a person is an alcoholic, when they are not, would require that they be using alcohol excessively, without progression, increased tolerance, blackouts, and addiction. In other words, their drinking must be at least in the gray area. Would the headlines the following day in the Washington Post say, "Dr. Hennigan declares John Doe to be an alcoholic"? Would he be subjected to some surgical procedure leading to the loss of a limb or organ? No, the worst that would happen would be that I would recommend that he attend an AA meeting, try not drinking one day at a time, and suggest that we discuss his experiences in AA. Let me assure you that if he gets to AA and goes regularly, it would not be long before he and others would perceive that he was not an alcoholic. So what great tragedy resulted as a consequence of my incorrect diagnosis? Actually, no tragedy at all.

When you hear someone say, "I believe Mary drinks too much," or "I believe John drinks too much," the chances are that Mary and John are alcoholics. Why do I say this? I say it for two reasons.

Based upon my own experience of how people use alcohol, I have found, in the vast majority of cases, that when someone is described as drinking too much, he or she will usually be found to be an alcoholic. One of the most diagnostic questions one can ask of a patient is, "Do any of your friends or family members feel you drink too much?" If the answer is yes, regardless of the explanations given, the patient probably is an alcoholic. Why so? We are a drinking nation and the use of alcohol is socially acceptable; in fact, it is often a sign of being sophisticated to be able to hold one's liquor.

We are too tolerant about drinking behavior. Some years ago, I was at a party in Georgetown, and several of us were talking about drinking and alcoholism. Since I was known to be an alcoholic, a young woman said to me, "I wonder if my boyfriend is an alcoholic?" I said, "Yes, he probably is," and she said, "How can you say that when you don't know anything about him?" I said, "If you who know him so well are wondering about it, the chances are he is an alcoholic." As we talked, she revealed additional facts that made the diagnosis quite certain.

Please remember that when anyone describes another person's drinking as heavy drinking, problem drinking, binge drinking, or says, "I believe so-and-so drinks too much," statistically the diagnosis is alcoholism. You may test this by checking on people you described any of these ways five years ago, and finding out what their situation is now.

Let us now look at the real culprit of the four possible diagnoses referred to earlier. Diagnosis D. I say the patient is not an alcoholic when he is an alcoholic. This is the real problem; in fact, if it were not for this problem there would be no point to this book.

There can be no doubt that of chronic illnesses, alcoholism is one of the most treatable, but, in spite of this, it is perhaps the most poorly dealt with. This is because alcoholics are seldom diagnosed until they are in an advanced stage; and often, when the diagnosis can be and should be made, it isn't.

To compound matters further, the one making the diagnosis often does not know how to get the patient to AA, so there the treatment falters. I will say more about this when I discuss treatment. Put aside your fears about the danger of saying "alcoholism" when the person is not an alcoholic. No nonalcoholic ever died because someone said he was an alcoholic, but many alcoholics have died because people feared saying "alcoholism."

5. DIAGNOSING ALCOHOLISM

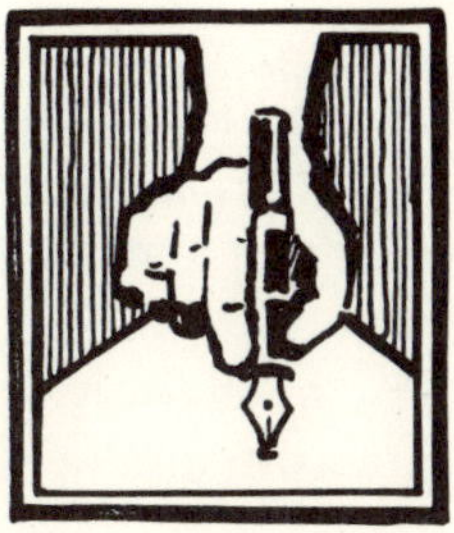

"If an idea presents itself to us, we must not reject it simply because it does not agree with the logical deductions of a reigning theory."

— Claude Bernard

One of the major problems regarding the treatment of alcoholism (as I have previously stated) has been a reluctance to make the diagnosis, because the term "alcoholism" is often seen as an accusation rather than as a diagnosis.

It is known that the patient doesn't recover from an illness unless it is treated; it isn't treated unless it is diagnosed; it isn't diagnosed unless it is looked for; and, of course, it isn't looked for unless it is known to exist.

Not much effort is made to establish the diagnosis because too many in the medical community feel alcoholism is not really a legitimate disease. One of my colleagues has said that, over the years, physicians never failed to ask him how much he smoked, but not one of them asked him how much he drank. As LeClair Bissell M.D. stated in *Alcoholism in the Professions,* "Two-fifths of doctors could not remember any colleague . . . saying anything critical about their drinking."

In my own experience, very few doctors showed an interest in how much I drank, and if I told them the amount, it was ignored. You may remember that my medical record of 1963 showed I drank a fifth of whiskey a day; yet no one discussed alcoholism with me.

Several years ago, I spoke on alcoholism with two doctors. One doctor in the audience said quite angrily, "You can't make the diagnosis of alcoholism, because alcoholics don't tell the truth about how much they drink." My response was that, in my experience, the doctor who so states doesn't know how to take a proper alcohol history. One of the panelists later said, "Leo, I didn't know you were such a street fighter!"

Mistaken ideas about diagnosing alcoholism are still prevalent; I hope to dispel these ideas.

Last year, I saw a program about alcoholism on a local television network, and several incidents in it illustrated the problems regarding diagnosis. In one instance, an attractive young woman who had regularly come to the emergency room because of her alcoholism was being interviewed by a doctor who was making rounds with her medical students. The doctor asked the patient if any other doctor had ever asked her about her drinking, and the woman said no. It was unfortunate that the physicians who had seen her had missed the boat, but more was to come. One of the students said, "If you had been asked, how much do you drink, would you have told the truth?" Another put-down for the patient. How much the alcoholic drinks is only a small part of the total examination.

The other incident had to do with a doctor at the National Institute of Health (N.I.H.) who was showing a method to diagnose alcoholism by very sophisticated laboratory tests. My concern was that his demonstration could indicate that alcoholism is difficult to diagnose. Diagnosis is a simple procedure.

DIAGNOSIS DISCOVERY:
Alcoholism as a Love Affair

Over the years in AA, I have been impressed with how many alcoholics, in telling about their alcoholism, begin with: "I am John, an alcoholic. I had my first drink when I was 17."

Most of these people, telling their story, seemed to remember their first drink, but, what was more interesting, they seemed to remember it with very positive feelings. As a result of this, I began to wonder, "Do alcoholics remember their first drink experience differently than nonalcoholics?"

In 1980, when we were having a conference on alcoholism in Baltimore, it was decided that some of the articles for our monthly medical journal would be written by alcoholic doctors. I mentioned my theory to Dr. Maxwell Weisman, a well-known authority on alcoholism, and he suggested I write it up.

My theory (previously mentioned) was that if alcoholics, more than nonalcoholics, were likely to remember their first drink, and if they revealed a different emotional reaction to the first drink than did nonalcoholics, perhaps this could be used as a diagnostic test. Also mentioned previously, I interviewed 50 alcoholics, 25 men and 25 women, and 50 nonalcoholics, also 25 men and 25 women. I simply asked the question, "Would you tell me all you can remember about your first drink."

My article on this was in the *Maryland State Medical Journal* in October 1980. This study made it clear that there was a remarkable difference between alcoholics and nonalcoholics regarding their memory concerning their first drink; but, more remarkable, was the emotion shown.

Alcoholics are more likely to have instant recall when asked about their first drink and remember far more details than do the nonalcoholics.

They have more positive feeling about the first experience with alcohol, and describe it in terms of fun, joy, even if, as happened with a few, objectively the experience was bad.

To many alcoholics, it would seem, the first experience with alcohol was one of the most significant events in the alcoholic's life.

The alcoholic's feeling about the first drink did not diminish with time.

Nonalcoholics, if they remembered their first drink, would describe their feelings about it with as much enthusiasm as if telling about the first time they tasted string beans.

The difference between alcoholics and nonalcoholics regarding their first drink was one of the most interesting and exciting moments I experienced as a physician.

This question I feel is diagnostic and the results led me to my concept that alcoholism can be seen as a love affair. Let me tell you of some of the responses relating to the love affair with alcohol.

Last year I saw an 83-year-old man for the first time. When I asked him to tell me all he remembered about his first drink, he immediately began smiling and said, "I was 17; Mr. Jones asked me to try his homemade wine; I liked it and drank so much I got drunk and my father had to carry me home."

Shortly after I wrote this paper, two other doctors and I (we were all in AA) visited a doctor whose name had been given to the Committee for Rehabilitation of Physicians. This man was 65, severely depressed, his abdomen distended; he was pale and in terrible condition. When I asked him if he could tell me all he remembered about his first drink, he became very alert. He began smiling and said, "Oh, yes, I was 15, on a farm in Texas; this horse wrangler asked me if I would like a drink, and I said OK and he reached in the bale of hay and pulled out a bottle. . . ." If you had been there and watched this demonstration, let me assure you, you would know you were observing a man talking about a love affair with alcohol.

Several years ago I was asked to see a 16-year-old girl who was very depressed. This was before I had written my article on first drink reactions. However, when I said to her, "If we had a fifth of whiskey here, how long do you think it would take for you to finish it?" She began smiling and said, “I could do it, but it would probably take all day.” Her depression seemed to vanish when alcohol was mentioned.

I was telling a friend of mine in AA about this test, and he began smiling and said, “I don’t remember my first drink, but I remember the first time I got drunk.” Actually this is just as valid as his remembering his first drink.

In my study of 50 alcoholics, 23 by their own evaluation felt they had never drunk normally -- and, I counted two more who misjudged their drinking.

Let me tell you some of the responses I had, and remember that these are immediate responses. The most important thing to note: it is not the remembering or not remembering that is significant, but rather how the person talks about the incident or about alcohol.

Male Nonalcoholics

1. “I hated the taste; I didn’t like it.” (age 31)
2. “I never liked it.” (age 52)
3. “I didn’t like it.” (age 62)
4. “It tasted like kerosene.” (age 43)
5. “It didn’t taste good.” (age 27)
6. “I didn’t like it.“ (age 64)
7. “No particular feeling one way or another.” (age 36)
8. “I didn’t like it.” (age 79)
9. “No particular feeling.” (age 55)
10. “I didn’t like it.“ (age 26)

Female Nonalcoholics

1. “I got sick on wine at 8, never drunk.” (age 35)
2. “I first drank on my 18th birthday -- one glass of wine -- no feeling one way or another.” (age 41)
3. “I had my first drink at 35 and never really liked it.” (age 71)

4. "I had my first drink at 16, no particular feeling, tried beer but I didn't like it." (age 57)

5. "I had a glass of wine as a child on holidays, but no particular feeling about my first drink." (age 53)

6. "I was about 16 or 17. It made me feel good, but I didn't like it." (age 45)

7. "I was about 10. I tasted sauterne and was disappointed at the taste." (age 59)

8. "About three years ago, I had a rum and coke and didn't like it." (age 20)

9. "At 10 or 11, I tried wine or beer and didn't like it." (age 33)

10. "I tasted an Old-Fashioned at 17 and didn't like it." (age 46)

In number six, note how the nonalcoholic didn't like it, even though it made her feel good. All the previous twenty answers by non-alcoholics were given in a very bland manner.

Male Alcoholics

1. "I was 17, it was bourbon. I liked the feeling it gave me." (age 24)

2. "I was 15. It was probably a Friday night. I got a six-pack and got drunk. My friends never said, 'Let's drink.' They always said, 'Let's get drunk.'" (age 37)

3. "I was 13, with a friend, had two or three drinks and got roaring drunk. From the word go I wanted to be euphoric." (age 23)

4. "It's a long story. I got drunk the first time and planned my next drink six months later." (age 59) He also remembered the girl's name, the hotel, and the name of the orchestra.

5. "I had beer at six, and when I was twelve I toasted the bride and that ended my social drinking. I stole a bottle of champagne and got drunk." (age 46)

6. "I was about 16, and I got it from a bootlegger. I was gagging and my eyes were tearing, and I was saying, 'God, that's good.'" (age 69)

7. "I had a beer at 12, liked the taste. Next time was when my parents were away, and I had two beers and half a bottle of wine. My first blackout was at 13, and I was in AA at 14." (age 21)

8. "I had my first drink at about age 15 at my sister's wedding and for the first time felt comfortable with myself and others." (age 43)

9. "At 17, I drank bourbon and liked the feeling it gave." (age 24)

10. "At age 12. There were four of us. Someone found a few cans of beer and it tasted damn good." (age 50)

Note, in number 6, an objectively unpleasant experience is seen as good to the alcoholic.

Female Alcoholics

1. "Maybe at six. It was interesting. In college I liked the taste and effect." (age 33)

2. "It was at the Olney Inn when I was 16, bourbon and ginger ale. My first blackout was in my twenties." (age 52)

3. "I was 16 and got drunk and had a blackout." (age 40)

4. "The first drink was in college; I got drunk on dandelion wine and made an ass of myself and did crazy things." (age 69)

5. "I was 16 and it was delicious. I drank as much as I could get." (age 27)

6. "I had champagne as a child and loved it -- at 11 or 12 I was more aware it could make you silly." (age 41)

7. "I was 16 at a club in Georgia. I was soon liking beer and got drunk often. No one had to twist my arm." (age 34)

8. "I remember it absolutely. I was 15, I was in someone's kitchen. It was delightful because my nose tingled. I couldn't wait to try it again." (age 63)

9. "I was 14. It was the fourth of July and there was a party with my parents. The noise was different and I was unsteady on my feet, but I liked it." (age 28)

10. "I was 13 and drank Seagram's out of a bottle and got drunk. I got drunk a week later." (age 26)

Number 9 is another example where an experience which would be seen as unpleasant to a nonalcoholic was perceived as positive by the alcoholic.

Let me assure the reader that the difference in the way the nonalcoholic talks about his first drink, or for that matter about alcohol in general, is vastly different from the way the alcoholic talks about it.

DETAILS ON DIAGNOSING TECHNIQUES

I have discussed this concept with many non-professionals, and they try it on their friends who drink too much, and they are pleased with the accuracy of this technique.

A physician, psychologist, social worker, nurse, or health specialist does not merely ask this question and stop there. No, it is the beginning of a technique of taking an alcohol history, starting right at the beginning and working up to the present. As you interview your patients, you will modify the questions to suit your personality and approach. After the first question, I say, "Did you get drunk the first time you drank?"

If the answer is yes, I ask, "Did you have a blackout?" I will explain that a blackout is a situation in which you were drinking and appeared in good condition, but the following day you couldn't remember everything.

When the answer is no to the question of getting drunk, I will ask, "How long was it after your first drink before you got drunk the first time?"

By talking about getting drunk and having blackouts, you help communicate the idea to the alcoholic of "doesn't everyone?" You help him feel more comfortable during the interview.

You will soon begin to note the difference between how alcoholics and nonalcoholics respond to these questions. The alcoholic is not upset by questions about being drunk or having blackouts, and the nonalcoholic will usually make it clear by his reaction that he is not alcoholic.

For example, if a nonalcoholic (let's say at this point I don't know this) is asked, "Did you get drunk the first time?" or, "How long after your first drink was it before you got drunk?" he will probably say, "Oh, I don't get drunk." I would then probably say, "You mean you never got drunk?" and if he said, "Never," or "Only once and never again," with obvious distaste, you would know you are dealing with a nonalcoholic.

You see, alcoholics accept getting drunk and having blackouts as par for the course. After all, isn't that why one drinks!

I emphasize that how the person talks about drinking will usually help you make you diagnosis. I know three physicians, a Frenchman, a Jew, and an Italian; all three have had one blackout and none of them is an alcoholic. If you were to watch them talk about their experience of one blackout, hearing their voices and watching their-faces, you would have no problem in knowing these were not alcoholics. They talk of their one blackout with, "My God, how could it have happened," and "Oh boy, never again," and I can assure you this is not how alcoholics talk of it.

The diagnosis is made on how the person talks about this experience with alcohol. In other words, the effect the alcohol has on him. After you ask a few questions about the first drink, first drunk, the first blackout to about ten alcoholics and ten nonalcoholics, it will soon become clear to you who is and who isn't an alcoholic.

Now that you have your patient talking about alcohol, you should then develop his use of alcohol in a chronological way. This is simply done by asking him how his drinking progressed; when, if ever, he began having difficulty with his drinking.

If you perceive a patient is not an alcoholic after asking about the first experience with alcohol; how many times if any the patient has been intoxicated; whether or not the patient has had blackouts, you can then ask him about his current drinking habits. If he does drink in a manner that you know to be social drinking, you know you are dealing with a nonalcoholic. This technique really helps you decide quickly whether a patient is or is not an alcoholic.

If you feel the person is an alcoholic, or may be, you then proceed by asking the patient to tell you about the change in drinking habits from the beginning of drinking to the present. Another good feature of this approach is by having the patient begin with telling about his early drinking, he is talking about the times which he saw as pleasant, joyful, and free of problems related to his drinking, so he is more inclined to be open about his drinking. Where appropriate, you may ask questions about missing work on Monday, having D.W.I.s (driving while intoxicated), accidents related to drinking, problems on the job, problems with the family, and so forth.

My method certainly is not the only method, and I don't say it is the best one; I simply say it is a way which I feel has merit and is not meant to exclude other ways of questioning the patient; it is to be used as an adjunct.

I have found that asking about the first drink is the best method of making an early diagnosis of alcoholism; alcoholism is no different from any other illness in that the earlier the diagnosis, the better the prognosis -- a point I continuously emphasize.

The shorter the time a person has been an alcoholic, the better the chance for discussing if he has a problem with alcohol.

In my case, I was never drinking normally. Proper questioning could have elicited the fact that I was, in stages, exhibiting early signs of alcoholism by:

1) occasional relief drinking;

2) drinking to handle shyness, loneliness; and

3) upping my tolerance for alcohol.

On the subject of early diagnosis, I have for years focused on two things:

1) Abnormal drinking, and

2) Effect; that is, the effect of alcohol on the patient.

In this regard, I would like to tell you about two patients I treated where the diagnosis was made very early.

I was treating a 24-year-old male who spoke of having three to five beers a night, never getting drunk, but speaking of his beer in a much more positive way then does a normal drinker. This was before I had done my study, and I was reluctant to say "alcoholism," but I did indicate he was getting to like it too much and should be aware of it.

Treatment ended, but two years later he called me, while having a severe anxiety attack. When I saw him the following day, it was clear that he was an alcoholic; his drinking had progressed rapidly in two years.

He began attending AA meetings and made a very good recovery.

Another patient was a 30-year-old man whom I saw because of a marital problem. During the first session, I asked him how much he drank (I had not yet developed my new technique), and he said "Oh, I have a few beers after work to get ready to face the wife." I indicated that, since his father was an alcoholic and he was beginning to depend on it, it would do no harm to go to some AA meetings and see how he felt about AA. The next week when he walked into my office, he said,"Leo, I think I'm in the right place (AA)."

This is an example of a person being open to visiting AA when their alcoholism is new. To repeat an important point, the earlier the diagnosis, the better chance for successful treatment. And of course it debunks the notion that alcoholics must hit some kind of bottom before treatment.

The late Dr. John G. Lofft, a psychiatrist, who was an authority on alcoholism and a consultant at Walter Reed Medical Center, wrote to me and made the following points:

> *Dear Leo,*
>
> *I would like to report my findings on the use of your clinical sign over the past two years. I well remember your teaching me how to elicit "Hennigan's sign" at the American Psychiatric Association meeting in May, 1983.*
>
> *I was able to carry this into practice and elicit the sign in my examination of alcoholic patients.*
>
> *I cannot tell you exactly how may patients I have tested for this sign, but it is likely several dozen.*
>
> *The response is always instant, and the swiftness,*

ease, and utility of this sign gives the clinician a time-saving screening device. In situations where there is no time, it can serve as an almost immediate marker of trouble.

I teach psychiatric residents at the Walter Reed Army Medical Center. In the last two years, I have taken some pains to teach your sign to residents as part of sharpening their diagnostic skills in the early diagnosis of alcoholism.

I hope other clinicians will evoke this sign and incorporate it into their practice.

With kindest regards,
John G. Lofft, M.D.

You may remember my comment that in medical circles it has been an unwritten and unspoken law that "Thou shalt not diagnose alcoholism in its early stages."

We must focus again and again on early diagnosis. In the June 19, 1985, edition of *Medical Tribune*, Dr. Richard Moore, internist at Johns Hopkins Hospital, stated that physicians are missing the diagnosis of alcoholism at least half the time.

Hopkins' commitment to the "major public health problem" makes it "the only academic center that has decided to take on the issue in all aspects."

Louis Wall, senior counselor of Hopkins hospital services, estimates that 35 percent of the 38,000 patients were alcoholic but fewer that five percent were so diagnosed.

Vanderbilt University and Harvard University are also becoming more aware of the need for early diagnosis of alcoholism.

Now that we are beginning to accept the early diagnosis of alcoholism, we can use this simple technique of asking about the first drink.

Remember, the alcoholic gets treatment when the doctor asks the right questions. For the word, "doctor," you may, of course, substitute the word psychologist, social worker, nurse, father, mother, son, daughter, friend, employer, etc.

Try it. I assure you it works.

6. ALCOHOLISM: A DISEASE OF PREJUDICE

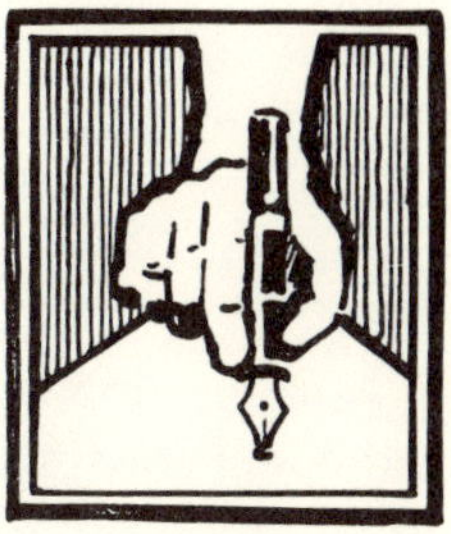

"Progress is impossible without change and those who cannot change their minds cannot change anything."

— George Bernard Shaw

There is a saying in medicine that if you can't treat an illness, classify it. This is a fancy way of saying, the less effective we are in treating an illness, the more there is written about it. Much has been written about alcoholism in recent years. So much writing indicates that alcoholism is still not treated effectively. According to the National Library of Medicine in Bethesda, Maryland, there are 1,565 books on alcoholism and 24,992 articles on alcoholism that have been written since 1966.

As I began to think of the problems related to treating alcoholism, and other diseases, I asked myself: "What is needed to deal effectively with any illness?" We, medical practitioners, need to know:

1) Causes of the illness;

2) An easy method of diagnosis; and

3) A simple, inexpensive, effective treatment.

I then asked myself, "How does this apply to alcoholism?" I detected a paradox, because:

1) To treat alcoholism effectively, we don't need to know its cause.

2) Contrary to popular opinion, alcoholism is extremely easy to diagnose.

3) There is a simple, effective treatment available to any who wish to recover from alcoholism, and it is called Alcoholics Anonymous (AA).

So here is the paradox: we have an illness the causes of which need not be known for successful treatment; an illness which is easy to diagnose; and an illness which has a simple, effective treatment. Why then is alcoholism still our number one health problem!

At this point in the mystery, I began asking myself, "Why, with all the studies which have been done, research which has been conducted, articles and books written, publicity on radio and TV, organizations such as M.A.D.D. and S.A.D.D., prominent people going public to talk of their alcoholism, why is it still our number one health problem?"

My thinking then led me to ponder over situations in areas totally unrelated to illness. While puzzling over this, a few thoughts started to come through to me -- could we be missing the boat by looking in the wrong direction, could there be some simple explanation we are overlooking? Could I, by utilizing the AA principle of "Keep it simple," have a better chance of finding the key to this mystery than by other approaches?

Detaching myself from the field of medicine one evening, I was reading a book on bridge by Dorothy Truscott, well known and recognized as an outstanding bridge player in New York. In the book, she was teaching how to determine the location of a certain key card in order to determine which opponent had this card. The successful making of one's bid was predicated upon the player's ability to determine which opponent held that card.

I then began thinking of the game of chess, particularly since Karpov and Kasparof were playing for the chess championship of the world. If you follow a chess game, you will find that, as the game proceeds, more and more attention is focused on one of the squares on the chess board, and the player who controls that will usually win the game.

My thoughts then turned to war, since, in a sense, we are waging a war against alcoholism, and then, more specifically, to individual battles. In my mind, I went back a few years to New Year's Day, when Sonia and I went to Gettysburg and, on a guided tour, heard the battle of Gettysburg described. As in a game of bridge or chess, if we read about enough battles, we begin to see a pattern where ultimate victory often is determined by one situation, one bridge, one hill, one crossroads, one specific entity.

With all these examples, I then asked myself, "Could there be one main feature about alcoholism we are missing, one fly in the ointment, one missing card, one square on the chessboard, one bridge in a battle?" With all the information we have about alcoholism, are we missing, or not adequately dealing with, the most important feature of the illness?

Then it occurred to me what was missing, or at least ignored, in the equation. The answer is simple. I'm sure you'll agree as you follow this example. I am going to ask you to imagine that there are 10,000 diseases. We are going to divide them into two groups, Group A and Group B.

In Group A, there are 9,999 diseases, and in Group B one -- alcoholism.

Why this strange classification? In Group A, the doctor makes the diagnosis, but in Group B, the patient is expected to make his own diagnosis.

The only illness in which a patient is expected to make his own diagnosis is alcoholism! He is not only expected to make his own diagnosis but, like a penitent during the Middle Ages, standing in front of a cathedral, the alcoholic is expected to admit he is an alcoholic. Have you ever heard anyone say, "You can't treat a diabetic unless he admits he is a diabetic; you can't treat a cancer patient until he admits he has cancer?" In fact, have you ever heard any illness referred to in terms of expecting the patient to admit the illness?

Now let us focus on the word "admit." I don't know what comes to your mind when you read or hear the word "admit," but when I hear or read the word, I think of murder, rape, incest, treason, espionage, bank robbery, etc. -- in other words, some type of criminal activity. When we use the word in relation to alcoholism, I am forced to ask the question, "What is the crime?" People use the word "admit" with alcoholism as casually as we use the word "ham" with eggs, and "apple pie" with America.

Why am I so certain? Simply because I have, over the years, asked numerous people what they knew about two diseases -- alcoholism and another I happened to think of at the time -- and I have never heard anyone use the word "admit" regarding other illnesses, but in practically every case, the word "admit" was used when questioned as to what is necessary in order for the alcoholic to be successfully treated.

The alcoholic is expected to admit he is an alcoholic; immediately give up the addiction and with the instincts of a homing pigeon, get to an AA meeting; and never again take a drink. Nothing unrealistic about our expectations for the alcoholic, is there?

If perchance the alcoholic does achieve some period of sobriety and then has a relapse or exacerbation of his illness (in AA it's called "a slip"), he can then be expected to be referred to with such sage comments as, "You can't trust an alcoholic," or, "You can't depend on alcoholics." What have "trust" and "depend upon" got to do with an illness? They are in the same category as the word "admit."

Let us look at two common chronic conditions and how they are treated. I have had personal experience with both of these -- hypertension and obesity.

Over the years, I have had moderate hypertension, at times treated with medication. Recommendations to me have been lose weight, get exercise, and cut down on salt.

With all of these, I have had difficulty; my level of enthusiasm and ability to follow directions have varied greatly over the years. Physicians, family members, and friends have always been understanding about my problem with cutting down on salt and with exercising. It has been a long struggle characterized by remissions and exacerbations, this being what we expect of a chronic condition.

Since returning from Hawaii in 1956, I have had trouble with my weight, which means I've been struggling with it for 30 years. I have had various periods of success, having tried Overeaters Anonymous, Weight Watchers, diet workshops, fads. But again, as regarding my hypertension, I have had great tolerance shown by physicians, friends, and family. This condition has also been characterized by periods of remission and exacerbation.

The same could be told regarding attitudes concerning ulcer patients, smokers, arthritics, in fact, any chronic condition. But please note how different our attitude is toward the alcoholic, how little tolerance we show, and how much we expect of him. We have unreasonable expectations of patients suffering from only one particular illness, and that illness is alcoholism.

We expect the alcoholic to accept a diagnosis which means he will be expected to admit "I am a no good, irresponsible, s.o.b.," because the alcoholic is still seen as something less than a sick person. In case you haven't yet realized why alcoholism is our number one health problem, it is because of the very simple fact that alcoholism is a disease of prejudice.

At this point, your reaction may be one of, "Big deal, this is what you've been leading up to? I've known that all along."

Have you really? That is, have you really realized the vast implications of what prejudice has done in dealing with this illness? Dealing with prejudice is very difficult because by its very nature it is not amenable to reasoning. Prejudice regarding alcoholism is so deep-seated and so much an integral part of the belief system of our society that to begin to deal with it effectively is as difficult as trying to pick up mercury with a fork.

Perhaps if I show the far-reaching consequences of our prejudice regarding alcoholism, it will help the reader to bring his own views into focus. Please remember that prejudice leads to these conditions;

it is not the other way around -- they do not lead to prejudice. Where prejudice is widespread, as is prejudice regarding alcoholism in our society, the rightness or wrongness of a belief is seldom questioned; we grow up believing certain principles to be facts.

Here is my list of the consequences of our prejudice about alcoholism:

#1. Alcoholism is the only disease in which the patient is expected to make the diagnosis.

#2. It is the only disease in which the word admit is freely used.

#3. It is the only disease in which the recovered patient may be referred to as reformed.

#4. Not only was alcoholism recognized as a disease in the 18th century, but alcoholism has been declared an illness by many medical groups.* However, large numbers of Americans in every walk of life do not accept alcoholism as a disease.

#5. Approximately 25 percent of patients in general hospitals are patients who are alcoholics, and yet their alcoholism is usually ignored.

#6. From my recent survey of medical schools and from my correspondence, I deduce that, in many medical schools, alcoholism is dealt with inadequately. Recently I was talking with a young doctor, a 1984 graduate, who said he received about two hours of instruction concerning alcoholism, our number one health problem, during his four years in medical school.

#7. Daniel R. Cloutier, Ph.D., an authority on alcoholism programs and one-time government advisor on substance abuse, cites a high percentage of alcoholism among the homeless. Referring to *A Report to the Secretary on the Homeless and Emergency Shelters* of the Office of Policy Development and Research of the U.S. Department of Housing and Urban Development, he indicates that among people who use emergency shelters in the U.S., 38 percent have a problem with alcohol or other drugs. This is significant because a pamphlet put out in Washington, D.C., by the Community for Creative Non-Violence, a well known organization working with Washington homeless, mentions medical clinic, infirmary, mental ..... .

---

* The American Medical Association, the American Psychiatric Association, the American Public Health Association, the American Hospital Association, the American Psychological Association, the National Association of Social Workers, and the World Health Organization

health counseling, dental clinic, etc., among their services, but until just recently, no mention was made of services to alcoholics.

The California Legislature Senate Office of Research, in its paper on *Shelter and Services: Solutions to the Burgeoning Crises of Homelessness* (1985), reports that the mentally ill homeless are the subject of a number of pending bills; and that approximately four bills have been introduced to provide services to the mentally ill homeless. The report quotes one California study as estimating that "38 percent of the homeless are 'chemical dependents' (primarily alcohol). . . ." The report goes on to state, however, that "no bill currently pending before the legislature names this target group (chemical dependents) as its focus."

I testified at a Veterans Administration hearing concerning an officer who obviously died of alcoholism, but his wife never collected compensation because alcoholism was never mentioned in his record. Fortunately, a doctor who treated him many years ago came forward and said, "The patient and I had agreed not to discuss his alcoholism." The doctor had been going along with the system which saw alcoholism, not as a disease, but as a moral issue. It took courage on his part to come forth as he did.

Some years ago I was treating a Roman Catholic nun who was an alcoholic and did well in AA. I could get little cooperation from the other 10 nuns in her convent. What did I want? I wanted to meet with them and help them to understand alcoholism. They were not interested. Can you imagine not receiving their help if I had been treating her for diabetes or any other "respectable" disease and needed their cooperation?

#8. The families of alcoholics are less cooperative than the families of other patients I have treated over the years. They -- and not the alcoholics -- have presented more problems for me.

#9. In most illnesses, we wish to make an early diagnosis. With alcoholism, our attitude is the alcoholic must first hit some kind of mystical bottom. This is of course pure nonsense, as the alcoholic gets well when the doctor or meaningful person in his life gets motivated. Can you imagine a doctor saying, "Mrs. X, you have a tumor in your breast which is malignant. When it metastasizes to your lung and liver, we will begin to treat it"?

I will not burden you with more examples of what prejudice leads to in terms of alcoholism. In order to understand and deal effectively with alcoholism, you must understand that prejudice is the key to the whole mystery of why alcoholism remains our number one health problem. It is the square on the chessboard, the missing card, the important bridge battle.

If you can see this, you can deal with the rest. If you can't deal with or accept the concept of prejudice in alcoholism, you will simply continue to adopt the philosophy, "I've already made up my mind; please don't confuse me with the facts."

7. THE TEACHING OF ALCOHOLISM IN MEDICAL SCHOOLS

"I never give them hell, I just tell the truth and they think it is hell.

— Harry S. Truman

Since we are dealing with our number one health problem, and since physicians in AA refer to alcoholism as the 4-2-1 disease, I would like to discuss the results of my survey on how alcoholism is taught in medical schools.

The concept of 4-2-1, regarding alcoholism, means that in four years of medical school, two hours are spent teaching about our number one health problem. In the excellent book, *Alcoholism in the Professions* by LeClair Bissell, M.D., and Paul Haberman, there are some interesting quotations by doctors who are alcoholics:

> *Only 11 percent of doctors in AA had ever heard AA mentioned as part of their training.*
>
> *Two-fifths of doctors could not remember any colleague or superior saying anything critical about their drinking.*
>
> *Usually the patient tells little or nothing about drinking and the treating person would not ask about it.*
>
> *Time and effort was wasted in trying to understand the reason for drinking.*

Let me repeat what I previously mentioned, that, in the medical community it is an unwritten law: "Thou shalt not diagnose alcoholism in its early stages."

Most physicians see themselves as not qualified to deal with this illness and my own experience bears this out. What is currently being taught to medical students about alcoholism?

With this in mind, I wrote a letter to the dean of every medical school in the United States and Canada. This is the letter I sent:

Dear Dean:

I am writing this letter with the hope that you will be able to help me regarding a book I am writing about our number one health problem -- ALCOHOLISM.

I graduated in 1950 from Georgetown University School of Medicine and am a psychiatrist and recovered alcoholic, having been active in Alcoholics Anonymous since 1963. The physicians in AA, both of my generation and younger doctors, all emphasize how little time was spent on teaching about alcoholism in medical school. In my book, I will be referring to this and am writing to the deans of all medical schools in the U.S. and Canada in order to obtain some information as to how much time is devoted to teaching medical students about alcoholism.

Because this is such a sensitive area, it is my promise to you, and this letter insures that any information given me will be treated totally anonymously; that is, nothing I mention will in any way be identified as having come from a certain school, dean, or designate of a certain dean.

I am particularly interested in knowing whether or not you have physicians who are recovered alcoholics talk to your students, and whether or not attending a certain number of AA meetings is part of the students' curriculum; however, any information regarding how alcoholism is taught to students during their years in your medical school would be appreciated. Whatever information I receive from this study will be a small, but nonetheless very important, part of my book.

I want to thank you in advance for any information you give me regarding how alcoholism is taught in your school.

Sincerely,
Leo P. Hennigan, M.D.

I used this format for my survey for two reasons. First of all, it was my feeling that such a letter, promising anonymity, would bring not merely some dry statistics, such as hours spent in teaching about alcoholism, but also some feelings about the problems experienced in teaching about this illness. Secondly, I am not a researcher and thus am not qualified to do research in this area.

Letters were sent to the deans of 126 medical schools in the United States and 16 in Canada. The response far exceeded my expectations, not only in terms of the number who responded to my letter, but also the very evident concern they revealed about this problem.

Before I discuss the results of this survey, I would like to demonstrate how others who are working in this area see the problem. The concern by the medical community about how alcoholism is taught in medical schools led to articles about this subject. They appeared in three recent issues of the *Journal of Medical Education* (August 1, 1985, September 2, 1985, and January 3, 1986). I believe that quotations from these articles will help demonstrate this concern. In *Substance-Abuse Education in Medical School: Past, Present, and Future*, published in the September 2, 1985, Dr. Stephen A. Helwick, Assistant Professor of Family Medicine at Louisiana State University School of Medicine, states the following:

> *In 1970, the National Council on Alcoholism sponsored a conference on professional training in alcoholism to assess the existing "state of the art" in substance-abuse training in the nation's medical schools. . . . The conference participants concluded that education regarding alcoholism had been neglected in medical schools, although alcoholism had been called the number one public health problem in the United States.*

In discussing funding for substance abuse education, he continues: "Three out of 40 schools surveyed said that nothing was taught about substance abuse." Dr. Helwick also discusses the conclusions of a study done by Dr. Coggan and others, which appeared in the *Journal of Family Practice in 1981.*

> *Based on extensive reviews and descriptions, Coggan and colleagues in 1981 reported the following characteristics of curricula in substance abuse. . . . There was a strong focus on the*

> *biomedical manifestations of end-stage alcoholism and on the treatment of late medical complications. Scattered bits of information tended to lack integration. The clinical exposure was directed toward the endstage alcoholic, and this left students with a despairing attitude and a tendency to avoid substance abuse patients. Moreover, what little improvement there was in local treatment centers tended to be superficial. Finally, students were rarely being taught the skills necessary to identify patients who were at risk or to intervene at an early stage of the disease.*
>
> *Although a growing number of medical schools point out to their students that physicians are a high-risk group for substance abuse, only a few schools have addressed the deeper problem of preventing the development of substance abuse among physicians.*

In the August 1985 issue of the *Journal of Family Practice*, Mark J. Hanlon, Ph.D., illustrates the case further in his article, "A Review of the Recent Literature Relating to the Training of Medical Students in Alcoholism."

> *. . . While teaching about alcoholism is increasing, the training needs to be expanded even more. The focus of the training should be on experiential/ clinical approaches rather than on the more prevalent approach of using lectures in nonclinical settings and should be on changing medical students' attitudes so they will be more understanding of alcoholics and more optimistic about their treatment.*

In discussing medical students' knowledge about alcoholism, Hanlon continues:

> *. . . another authority had similar findings using a similar test on alcoholism developed by Weinberg. Medical students who attended an AA meeting (as a curriculum option) had higher scores than students who did not exercise that option. Even though the testing followed the AA attendance by two years.*

Dr. Hanlon concludes:

> *Alcoholism education continues to receive inadequate attention in medical training programs despite documented expansion of such education. The attitudes of medical students and residents toward alcoholism, alcoholics, and alcoholism treatment are the appropriate foci of education in this area and are best addressed through experiential/clinical avenues.*

In the January 1986 issue of the *Journal of Family Practice*, Richard D. Moore, M.D., and Faye E. Malitz describe the results of this lack of education on the ability of medical residents to diagnose alcoholism at an early stage. Their article, "Underdiagnosis of Alcoholism by Residents in an Ambulatory Medical Practice" states:

> *To assess the ability of residents to diagnose alcoholism, a survey was conducted of 95 patients from the ambulatory care internal medicine practice of the Johns Hopkins Hospital. . . . The questionnaire contained four questions, one each on cutting down on alcohol consumption, annoyance at criticism of alcohol consumption, guilty feelings about alcohol consumption, and use of alcohol early in the day. The answers to the questionnaire were compared with the residents' diagnoses of alcoholism on the medical record. Alcoholism was diagnosed by the residents in only 11 of the 20 patients (55 percent) who had given three or more yes answers on the alcoholism questionnaire and in only 14 of the 31 patients (45 percent) who had given two or more yes answers. (Yes answers indicate that patients suffer from alcoholism.)*
>
> *Alcoholism has been reported to affect from four percent to more than 20 percent of patients in primary care medical practices and in the general hospital setting. . . . Yet despite the prevalence of alcoholism, physicians typically learn to recognize alcoholism only when severe physical damage such as cirrhosis or pancreatitis has occurred and have minimal skills for diagnosing or managing alcoholism*

> *in its earlier stages . . . . As alcoholism advances, it becomes increasingly unlikely that intervention and treatment will succeed. At early stages, however, alcoholism is an illness that can be treated successfully. . . .*
>
> *. . . In summary, the results of the present study indicate a moderate underdiagnosis of alcoholism by residents in a major academic medical center. This finding suggests an important educational need. Given the high incidence of alcoholism and its effect on physical and emotional health, it is important that residents learn to diagnose alcoholism at an early stage of the disease.*

Let us now turn our attention to the results of the survey I conducted. There was obvious concern about how our medical schools deal with alcoholism. The attitudes shown were the same in both the U.S. and Canada.

A large number of respondees showed a definite interest in this survey and spoke favorably about it. Many offered valuable suggestions to me, sent me articles (one even sent a book of his on this subject), and many offered further information. One respondee not only wrote a very thorough letter, but several weeks later, sent me several articles which he felt I could use. Because my letter promised anonymity, many were extremely open about the teaching of alcoholism at their various schools. From the 126 schools in the United States, I received a response from 78, or 61.9 percent; and from the 16 schools in Canada, there were seven responses, or 43.7 percent.

Before discussing some critical letters, let me report the overall results of my questionnaire:

Q: How many medical schools had students attend at least one AA meeting?

A: 20 schools, mandatory; other schools, optional.

Q: How many had recovered alcoholic physicians talk to the students?

A: 39 (total from all schools reporting).

Q: Did the school have an elective course on alcoholism?

A: 38 did, but how many students took the elective varied -- one percent of the students took it; a few took it; four-to-five students took it; 15 students took it, etc.

Q: Approximately how many hours were spent teaching about alcoholism?
A: From two to 20 hours.

Q: How many schools were in the process of improving their current program?
A: 15.

I numbered each letter as I received it, and, in general, some of the most open comments came later, almost as if there were some soul-searching before the letter was written. In the order I received them, here are some comments from the letters:

> *Letter 3: It will not surprise you to hear that our school is like most other schools -- we devote relatively little time to the subject.*
>
> *Letter 24: I am sorry to say that we may not do as well as we should in teaching the subject to medical students. . . . It may not be enough but you can be certain that your letter has stimulated us to think about our curriculum and to consider whether or not new techniques of teaching should be added.*
>
> *Letter 31: We have not had a recovered alcoholic physician talk to our students. It is an excellent idea, and I have discussed it with our behavioral science course director.*
>
> *Letter 34: It is possible for students to graduate without really learning about alcoholism.*
>
> *Letter 37: There is no specific course on alcoholism any more than there is a specific course on depression. . . . Medical education is always delinquent in that it should offer more in many areas ranging from alcoholism through nutrition to virology.* (This letter and several other expressed a belief that students would learn more about alcoholism in postgraduate years. I regret to say I do not share their optimism.)
>
> *Letter 59: Part of the difficulty is that some of the basic science teaching is fragmented in the first two years among*

psychiatry, pharmacology, and internal medicine. The difficulty that arises is that there is inconsistency in the teaching of concepts and in some instances there is frank 'counterteaching.' A prime example is the concept that alcohol abuse is secondary to a deepseated personality problem versus the concept that it is a primary illness. There is a similar inconsistency regarding prognosis and treatment modalities. In internal medicine, for instance, it is acknowledged as a primary illness, but the prognosis is believed to be so poor, there is little active intervention taught at any level.

Letter 67: At most there may be two or three lectures in the required curriculum. . . . Overall I would say that we give very little time and exert very little effort in teaching our medical students about alcoholism.

Letter 75: This has been rather a long letter to tell you we are currently doing nothing.

Letter 77: There is a clinical elective in alcoholism in the fourth year of the curriculum (four weeks), but it is only rarely chosen.

Letter 81: At present the School of Medicine does not include a course specifically addressing the subject of alcoholism.

Letter 82: I am sure that more could be done, but this appears to me as an honest starting point! . . . I think we still need a comprehensive approach, where physicians are a significant part of the treatment teams.

Letter 85: As part of a selective program in our first year, students are offered a class in alcoholism. The usual enrollment is 15 students. (No other exposure to the teaching of alcoholism was mentioned in this letter.)

I have divided the 85 medical school responses into four groups reporting as follows: (A) An excellent program for teaching their students about alcoholism. (B) Fairly good program or are in the process of establishing such a program. (C) Poor program. (D) Vague answers; couldn't evaluate. Since many of the letters were narrative and not specific as to the number of hours used to teach about alcoholism, my putting a school into any of these groups is of necessity somewhat subjective. An example of a vague response: "I acknowledge receipt of your letter of June 13, 1985, and I thank you for writing to me." No other information was given.

To summarize 85 responses:

A. 10 schools had good programs;
B. 25 had fair programs;
C. 43 had poor programs; and
D. 7 were too vague to evaluate.

The number of students to become physicians in 1986 from these schools was as follows:

A. 1,484
B. 2,299
C. 4,563
D. 1,068

I believe that this survey demonstrates several things:

1. Some medical schools (10) have excellent programs for the teaching of alcoholism.

2. Other medical schools (15) are in the process of augmenting their programs.

The two most important teaching devices for this illness are being utilized more. These are: (a) attending AA meetings on the part of medical students; and (b) hearing physicians who are recovered alcoholics tell of their experiences with alcoholism.

4. Many letters indicate not complacency, but a strong desire to improve how the subject of alcoholism is taught.

5. On the negative side, there are still many medical schools where alcoholism is dealt with poorly, in some cases ignored.

This last point leads to the tragic conclusion that each year thousands of medical students become physicians knowing literally nothing about our number one health problem: alcoholism.

One solution to the problem of better medical education on alcoholism is two-fold: (A) Students should be taught alcoholism by a recovered alcoholic, preferably a physician or a qualified expert in the field. Three nonalcoholic authorities I personally know are Drs. Maxwell N. Weisman, Frank Cresswell, Jr., and Earl Mitchell. (B) The students must attend AA meetings.

"Last but not least, many members of Alcoholics Anonymous -- especially John B. and Bunny -- have taught me invaluable truths about alcoholism. Over the last ten years, I have attended about 50 AA meetings; I would recommend the same to any serious student of the disease. Perhaps no one understands alcoholism treatment as well as those who have overcome the illness in themselves."

— Dr. George E. Vaillant,
"The Natural History of Alcoholism"

I agree with Dr. Vaillant's recommendation that medical students should attend 50 AA meetings. However, I would say that all medical students should do this, not only the serious ones. Considering the magnitude of the problem, the prejudice in the professions and the educational benefits, 50 meetings in four years of medical school (about one per month) would seem to me an excellent use of student time. If this were put into effect now, I am certain that, in a few years, all medical students upon graduating, would be qualified to deal effectively with our number one health problem.

Concerning the teaching of alcoholism to medical students, I reviewed six standard medical textbooks to see how alcoholism is presented. In five books, the emphasis was on the later stages of alcoholism and how to deal with it. In the sixth, the writer emphasized the need for early diagnosis, but stated this was difficult because physicians' knowledge about early alcoholism was limited. The writer correctly pointed out that this has led physicians to ignore all but the most obvious of drinking problems. In five of the six books, AA was mentioned, but usually in a very bland way and never presented as the treatment of choice for the illness.

8. THE TREATMENT OF ALCOHOLISM

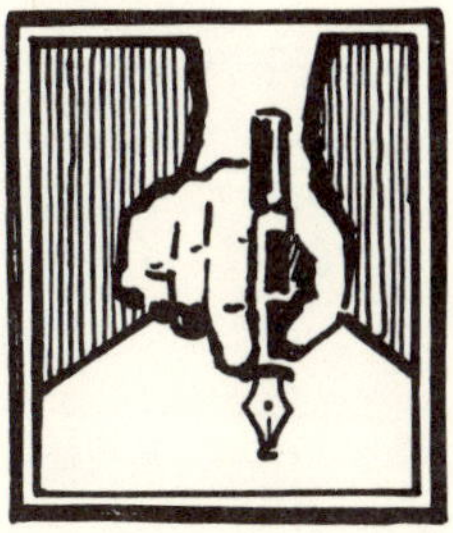

"You try to save a drowning man without prior authorization, and even if he resists you, you do not let him go, even when he tries to strangle you."

— Dag Hammarskjold
on UN actions in the Congo, 10/18/60

As the reader has probably concluded by now, my approach to the treatment of alcoholism is a very simple, pragmatic one: "What works?"

The answer has to be Alcoholics Anonymous since I know of no other treatment equal to AA in terms of results achieved. It is estimated that 50 percent of those who attend AA stop drinking immediately, and 25 percent more do so eventually. Considering that alcoholism has been progressing for years before the average alcoholic becomes involved in AA, a 75 percent recovery rate is phenomenal. Note, too, that prior to 1935 when AA began, very few alcoholics survived the illness.

Let me explore the hazards one experiences with therapists who have failed to learn enough about alcoholism. This group includes many physicians, psychotherapists, psychiatrists, psychologists, social workers and others who identify themselves as therapists. Be wary of them.

Here are my comments about therapists who "pussyfoot" about alcoholism and about AA. First I will list a therapist's possible statement or approach; then my response.

1. "Let's not discuss your drinking problem -- your alcoholism right now."

Obviously, the therapist is not comfortable about dealing realistically with problems related to drinking. He may know that the alcoholic is almost never ready to be confronted about his alcoholism, just as no one is ever ready to be confronted about a serious problem.

Immediate confrontation is necessary. This should be in the first session -- once you have made the diagnosis of alcoholism. This patient could easily be involved in an accident before a second session and kill himself or an innocent human being.

In confronting him or her, speak in positive terms; because actually the prognosis is better than for any other fatal illness.

I help the patient recognize the necessity of "looking into AA." I emphasize that AA could help him or her give up suffering.

One doesn't merely say, "You're an alcoholic"; it is necessary to demonstrate to the patient the progression of the illness and explain what the future will be.

I often let the patient know I will not comment on his drinking if he is willing to go to AA, because, in my experience, it may be traumatic to talk about giving up alcohol, but going to AA can be seen as not too unreasonable.

2. "You're not really an alcoholic."

This usually means the patient is an alcoholic, but the physician or therapist hasn't the courage to say so. Just as you can't be slightly pregnant, you can't be slightly alcoholic.

3. "Try to cut down on your drinking."

If there is one statement which clearly shows the doctor or therapist is incompetent in the area of alcoholism, it has to be this one. If there is anything the alcoholic can't do, it's to cut down on his drinking. Hasn't he been trying for years? When that is said, the only thing the patient hears is, "My doctor said it's all right for me to drink."

4. "AA is not the only treatment for alcoholism, and is not for everyone.

I quake when I hear this. Those who say it usually are negative about alcoholism, the alcoholic, and AA; and their prejudice is involved in this statement. The alcoholic has enough resistance to AA as it is. This statement enables him to try every other approach. Why? Because the alcoholic knows that AA is equated with not drinking, and if there's one thing the alcoholic doesn't want, it's to not drink.

If someone were to list 15 ways of treating alcoholism to include jogging, mountain climbing, yoga, AA, and psychotherapy, etc., you can expect most alcoholics would try everything else before trying AA. I'm being a bit facetious, but only a bit.

Also, beware of studies by people who are "going to help alcoholics drink normally." These studies get many alcoholics back to drinking, because, after all, "didn't Doctor X in his study show some alcoholics could return to normal drinking?" The fallacies are obvious because:

A. No alcoholic wants to drink normally, as drinking abnormally and getting drunk are what it's all about.

B. They are attempting to get a drug addict (alcohol is a drug) to use drugs normally.

C. The fact is that if it were possible to continue to use alcohol with any degree of success, someone in AA would have discovered how. We all spend a lot of time trying. In AA, we refer to these attempts as "Research."

As to "AA not being for everyone," let us imagine I had an illness which required surgical intervention, and I consulted a surgeon. He presented me with two types of surgical procedures: Procedure A which afforded me a 75 percent chance of survival, and Procedure B which afforded me a 5-10 percent chance of survival. What would be his responsibility if I chose Procedure B? I would certainly question his interest in me as a patient if he didn't do everything possible to convince me I should select Procedure A. Why then are so many doctors and therapists so glibly able to say AA isn't for everyone, and AA isn't the only treatment? I have my own opinion. I'll let you, the reader, decide upon yours.

5. "Let me prescribe a tranquilizer or sedative."

To treat an addictive person with a tranquilizer or sedative is dangerous; for an alcoholic, who may also suffer from anxiety, depression, or insomnia, could, through such medication, become addicted to the tranquilizer or sedative. You remember, when I asked my doctor for sedation, what happened to me.

I teach all my patients how to meditate and my approach is meditation, not medication. I've found that this approach, plus getting the patient to AA, works. If the patient is in need of hospitalization, however, I refer them to an appropriate colleague where they will be medicated on an in-patient basis.

6. "Let's find the underlying cause as to why you drink."

This of course is an exercise in futility, because those using this approach have no awareness that alcoholism is a primary disease and is not dependent upon one's psychological makeup. This procedure does immeasurable harm, because it promises something it can never deliver. The often unspoken promise is, "When we find out why you began drinking, your drinking will normalize," or, "When we know just why you drink, your drinking will normalize or cease."

The truth of the matter can best be shown in my own case. Sixteen years of psychotherapy were futile in terms of doing anything about my drinking. We, my doctors and I, were trying to find out after each drinking bout, why I drank. Eventually I managed on my own to reach certain conclusions:

— I drank when I was depressed,
but I drank if I were happy.

— I drank when I didn't get my promotion,
but I drank when I got my promotion.

— I drank when I was lonely,
but I drank when I wasn't lonely.

— I drank for despair,
and I drank for joy.

Eventually, I realized I drank for only one reason: I drank because I was a drug addict and alcohol was my drug. Believe me, it is just as simple as that.

Using psychotherapy to treat alcoholism is like treating diabetes with penicillin or pneumonia with insulin. I have no objection to using psychotherapy, provided the therapist is honest enough to know that AA is the treatment of choice for the alcoholic and is trying to get the patient into AA. I tell my patients that if they go to AA they are more likely to recover; if they attend AA, only 10 to 15 percent will also require my services for psychotherapy.

Alcoholism is a good area for unscrupulous therapists to function, because most alcoholics will be very happy never to have AA mentioned, and both patient and therapist can indulge in the fantasy they are doing something about the patient's "drinking problem."

During the initial part of therapy, my main goal is to focus on getting them adequately involved with AA. When my patients ask me how many nights a week they should attend AA, I ask, "How many nights a week did you drink?" Once they have several months of sobriety, I have them make a decision, usually with the help of their sponsor in AA, as to the number of meetings to attend. The more meetings attended the first year, the better the chance the alcoholic has of getting well.

Whenerver I see an alcoholic, I ask him or her to bring in some family member. Alcoholism is a family disease; the family members have their own problems related to being a mate or family member of an alcoholic. Ideally, I try to have the mate (or interested friend) go to AlAnon, the alcoholic to AA, and the children to Alateen.

Because of the nature of the disease, because it's a disease involving prejudice, the alcoholic is seen by society and his family, as being weak, no good, irresponsible, etc. Understandably, the alcoholic resists being called an alcoholic. To accept that diagnosis is to accept that he's no good.

In addition, the alcoholic is expected to give up his "best friend" (alcohol); in his confused mind, he finds this a horrible thought. To the alcoholic, life without alcohol would be unthinkable. Remember, when we are drinking, we are as confused about alcohol as one could be.

Let me try to explain what it is like to be an alcoholic:

— I felt shy -- I drank, my shyness vanished.

— I felt uncertain -- I drank, I had confidence.

— I felt lonely -- I drank, I felt accepted.

— I couldn't sleep -- I drank, I could sleep.

The list could go on and on, but I think you see what I mean. After this continues for years, the alcoholic has had thousands of such reactions. Can you see why we don't want to give up alcohol?

Now, after years when alcohol begins to do the opposite, can you reasonably expect us to believe it is the alcohol?

"There are two stages of alcoholism:

1 -- when it does something for you,

2 -- when it does something to you."

I was talking with a friend of mine who was an alcoholic counselor, but not an alcoholic. When we were discussing alcoholism, he said, "Leo, the one thing I can't really understand is why alcoholics hold so strongly to their wish to drink even when it's causing so much trouble."

I thought awhile and said, "Let me try to explain by giving you an example. Suppose you come to me with a certain medical condition which I diagnosed as 100 percent fatal and told you so. Suppose I told you there was one cure which was 100 percent effective. All you had to do to recover completely and have a long life was to give up sex completely forever." His jaw dropped! I said, "Now you know how an alcoholic feels when faced with giving up alcohol."

Regardless of how bizarre it sounds, the alcoholic cannot imagine living without drinking. Remember, he had many good times with alcohol; or at least he thought they were good times.

Since resistance is to be expected, it is necessary to use rather heroic measures in helping the alcoholic.

If there is one word which is most important in understanding why alcoholism remains our number one health problem it has to be the word --

PREJUDICE.

You must recognize that, regardless of how logical, rational, intelligent, lucid, competent, the alcoholic may be in many areas, when it comes to his being able to see his relationship to alcohol in a correct way, he is totally --

INCOMPETENT.

A word which is just as significant in terms of treatment, a word without which treatment seldom succeeds, the one word you must learn to understand and use successfully if you are to help any alcoholic, is the word --

CONFRONTATION.

There is the story about a man who bought a mule and asked the farmer what he had to do to have the mule work hard. The farmer said, "You've got to give him a lot of love." The new owner did so, but no work was done by the mule. He took the mule back and explained the situation to the farmer. The farmer picked up a two-by-four and hit the mule on the head, and the mule proceeded to work as desired. The owner said, "But you told me I had to give him a lot of love." "Oh, you do," said the farmer, "but first you have to get his attention."

With the alcoholic, you can also pull the rug from under him; or, put a gun (symbolically) to his head.

You remember the gun at my head occurred when Pete Sterrantino told me he heard my clinic was going to fire me. Had that occurred ten years sooner, in 1953, when I was in Ypsilanti, Michigan, instead of in 1963, I assure you I would have been in AA in 1953.

Some years ago, while with the Committee for Rehabilitation of Physicians, I talked with Jim, a surgeon, about his use of alcohol and drugs. He was clearly an alcoholic and drug addict, and I recommended hospitalization. He objected strongly; after he finished comparing me with the FBI and the Gestapo, he declared that he was not going to accept my advice.

I then stated that was OK with me; that I would inform the Peer Review Committee of his wishes and that the problem would then be between him and them. I also pointed out they were interested in seperating him from his license to practice medicine.

I mentioned there were federal people interested in him because of prescriptions he had written.

What was the outcome? --

INSTANT MOTIVATION.

Did Jim suddenly accept the status of being a drug addict and alcoholic? Did he have a desire to give up drugs and alcohol? Of course not. But he did accept my advice. Even if he didn't agree with me, or even if he were in a hospital, his joining an alcohol recovery group would be looked upon favorably by the Peer Review Committee. He was hospitalized, treated, did well, and not many months later was able to thank me and laugh about the incident.

Treatment begins once you confront the alcoholic, because, if done properly, his drinking is never again the same.

More often than not, I am not so fortunate to have such clout as having the medical society behind me while dealing with a doctor in a sensitive situation. When employers work with me and vice versa, it usually helps get the alcoholic well. When confronted with, "Do something about your drinking or you will lose your job," most alcoholics will go to AA.

Here I want to emphasize that no one comes to AA filled with joy. Usually, we come to AA depressed, scared, angry, bitter. It is only when we get there that we find it isn't at all what we thought it would be.

The notion that, once confronted, the alcoholic will immediately stop drinking and never have a relapse is ridiculous. Have you ever known of someone who, being confronted about obesity, immediately went on a diet, lost the appropriate amount of weight, and kept it off?

For example, after 30 years of trying to cut down on salt, I have been able, in the last two months, to eat without using a salt shaker.

Here's how to handle confrontation.

- Don't confront the alcoholic when he is under the influence of alcohol; do it when he is sober or sobering up.

- Don't confront by telling him he drinks too much, as that is merely an opinion. If I were told I drank too much, I would deny this, because, to me, one fifth a day was not too much; it was just the right amount for me.

- Confront him about the results of his drinking; how it affects his behavior. Tell him you are concerned about his behavior when he drinks, his poor driving, slurred speach, hostile behavior, missing work on Mondays. This he may understand.

- Above all, confront out of love and caring, not out of anger. We are sick people, we are hurting enough, don't attack us about something over which we have no control. All you do is give us another reason to continue drinking.

If possible, confront the alcoholic with another interested person or persons being present. Possibly you could offer to go to an AA meeting with him. When I confront the alcoholic, I point out the results of his drinking, but more important, I predict what the future will be if he continues to drink.

The main purpose of focusing on the unpleasant consequences of drinking is to help spoil his drinking. Remember, no alcoholic wants to stop drinking, he wants to stop hurting.

Let me assure you, if you confront the alcoholic appropriately, the results will usually follow, but not on your timetable.

I have a principle which will help you in this situation; in fact, it's a principle I teach to all my patients, alcoholic or otherwise. I call it the principle of DAR, which does not stand for Daughters of the American Revolution. It stands for:

Don't
Anticipate
Results.

Let me give you a few examples to demonstrate this, but before I do, let me say that years ago, if I told someone they were alcoholic, and they failed to stop drinking immediately, I thought I had failed.

I no longer am concerned about this because I have found I am very poor at predicting which alcoholics will get well immediately, eventually, or never. My concern is to do the right thing; and then it is up to the patient.

Several years ago, I was at an AA meeting, and a man came up to me and said, "You probably don't remember me, but you saw me once seven years ago, and told me I was an alcoholic, and I didn't accept it. I felt that, being a Jewish lawyer, I couldn't be an alcoholic, and since you were Irish and an alcoholic, you probably saw everyone as being alcoholic. You will be happy to know you were right, and I've been in AA four years."

A few years ago, I was at a medical meeting in Baltimore when I heard someone calling my name. It turned out to be Mary, a patient I had seen four years before. Two or three times I told her she was an alcoholic and recommended AA. She dropped out of treatment. Ten months later she called me, identified herself, and made an appointment to see me. She spent 10 months trying to prove she wasn't an alcoholic, only to find that she was. I had her hospitalized; she did well and required no further therapy with me since she was active in AA.

In telling both of these people they were alcoholic, I spoiled their drinking by focusing on the unpleasantness of their drinking and predicting what the future would be.

As I have stated previously -- and repetition is needed -- the earlier the diagnosis is made, or the shorter the period the person has been an alcoholic, the better the chance there is of their going to AA -- and recovering.

Upon its being recommended, some patients immediately go to AA and immediately stop drinking.

After the confrontation, you must allow the alcoholic to do his own "research" about his drinking. Just keep in mind the principle of DAR (Don't Anticipate Results).

You must treat the drinking before you treat other symptoms such as: depression, anxiety, fear, insomnia, impotence, loneliness, gastritis, hypertension, and suicidal thoughts. If drinking is treated successfully, this will lead to the improvement of the other conditions. The most efficient way for a therapist to learn the value of AA is by attending AA meetings personally.

I wrote an article, "Alcoholics Anonymous: Something of Value," which appeared as a reprint in the *Maryland State Medical Journal*, October 1980, in which I suggested that we think of the AA way of life as a substitute for drinking and as "something of value." Robert Ruark, in his novel, *Something of Value*, had this idea in mind, and I quote:

> *If a man does away with his traditional way of living and throws away his good customs, he had better first make certain that he has something of value to replace them.*
>
> — *Basuto Proverb*

Let me include some quotes from my article; and paraphrase other facts I presented.

". . . Perhaps now we should discuss how AA started and then compare treatment of the alcoholic before and after the beginning of AA.

"Back in the nineteen-thirties, Dr. Carl Jung stated he knew of only a few alcoholics who had recovered, and they were ones who had a religious experience; in essence, few alcoholics recovered.

"In 1935, a New York stockbroker, Bill W., an alcoholic, was in Akron, Ohio, on a business trip. He was tempted to drink and knew from past experiences the only way he could not drink was to talk with another alcoholic. From the church directory in his hotel, he chose the name of Reverend Walter Tunks, who gave him the names of 10 people to call who might be able to put him in contact with an alcoholic. He began calling them without success until he got to the last one: Henrietta Seiberling, who recently died at 91. She arranged his meeting with Dr. Bob, an alcoholic surgeon, who agreed to see Bill W. for 15 minutes. The following day, they met and talked for hours and out of this came AA. Bill W. and Dr. Bob were the co-founders.

"In 1939, those who had recovered realized that something very profound had happened and began to ask why they had recovered from an illness from which, previously, practically no one had recovered. You will note that AA did not develop in a scientific way. Rather than developing a theory and trying to prove it, alcoholics tried to do what they could to recover and also help other alcoholics. When they achieved success, they said, in essence, let us pool our knowledge; let us find out what was responsible for our recovery.

"The result was the book, *Alcoholics Anonymous*, known in AA as "The Big Book." It contains the stories of the first alcoholics in AA to recover and the principles which helped them. The first edition's preamble describes what AA is and lists the 12 suggested steps as guides to be followed if one wishes to recover from alcoholism."

At this point in the story it was my intention to quote from the book, *Alcoholics Anonymous*, the Preamble and the Twelve Steps of the AA Program. To this end a letter was sent to Alcoholics Anonymous World Services Inc. requesting permission to quote from this book. Permission was denied and their letter regarding this states "As guardians of the tradition the board will not approve the use of the material requested if there is a tradition violation involved ..."

The Preamble and the Twelve Steps from which I wanted to quote are just words, words that could heal, words that could help. As information is power, my desire was to share it with those in need.

I guess that if one believes that sharing information and words from a book that is readily available in the public library system, is a violation of tradition then this reprinting of their words would qualify. I might also add that the tradition is being violated because I am personally opposed to the continuing practice of anonymity and will discuss this in more detail later.

Having made this explanation I would like to give the reader the essence of the message contained in the Preamble and the Twelve Steps as follows:

Alcoholics Anonymous is an organization whose members have a common bond, that bond is their desire to stop drinking. The members, both men and women, act as a support group to anyone interested in doing something about their alcoholism. AA is a non-sectarian, non-political, self-supporting organization with an open membership policy. In order to help people suffering from alcoholism to recover the group follows a program which, in essence, states that:

- One cannot deal with this illness alone because of its very nature.
- One needs to self search from within and seek support from outside of self.
- To recover fully from this illness one needs to be aware of their shortcomings.
- One needs to recognize the hurt caused others and to have a desire to heal these wounds.
- One needs to continue to seek truth about self and accept the healing process recovery brings.
- It is recommended that we try to bring this information to the alcoholic who still suffers and to live life in accordance with these principles.

By 1976, there were conservatively one million people in AA. By 1979, there were over 33 thousand groups in over 90 countries.

From AA have come:

1. AlAnon and Alateen for the families of alcoholics.
2. Narcotics Anonymous.
3. Gamblers Anonymous.
4. Neurotics Anonymous.
5. Overeaters Anonymous.

"How does AA work?" is the most frequently asked question and is, classically answered, "It works just fine." I do not say this to be sarcastic or facetious, but only to indicate that perhaps we in AA probably spend relatively little time thinking about how it works. But it does. We emphasize AA is a program of action, not an analyzing process.

Alcoholism is a way of life, as is AA. The people in AA say your drinking life is filled with suffering; let us show you a happier way to live.

. . . .

Up to this point, I have focused mainly on the treatment of the alcoholic on an out-patient basis, but let me mention something about the alcoholic whose illness has progressed to where he requires hospitalization.

It is most important that the patient be detoxified in a setting which is particularly focused on dealing with alcoholism.

Everyone treating patients should know which physicians in the community are qualified to deal with the hospitalized patient, and it is a rare community now which doesn't have appropriate facilities for dealing with the hospitalized alcoholic.

There are two directories, available at most public libraries, which list appropriate centers for the in-patient treatment of alcoholism by state:

1. National Alcoholism Treatment Program Directory.
   Published by: U.S. Journal, Inc.
   1721 Blount Road, Suite 1
   Pompano Beach, Florida 33009
   (305) 979-5408

2. National Directory of Drug Abuse and Alcoholism Treatment and Prevention Programs.
   Published by: U.S. Department of Health and Human Services
   Publication No. (ADM)85-321
   National Institute on Drug Abuse
   National Institute on Alcohol Abuse and Alcoholism
   5600 Fishers Lane
   Rockville, Maryland 20857
   (202) 655-4000

Since getting the alcoholic in the hands of a qualified physician is essential, and since most physicians are none too qualified in this area, I have established a policy to handle this situation.

When asked how one can find a qualified physician, I have advised the interested family member to attend some AA or Al-Anon meetings and ask the members for names of physicians. This I have found to be as satisfactory a way as I know.

In recent years we have heard of prominent people going to various places for treatment of their alcoholism. These are basically hospitals which have a number of recovered alcoholics on the staff. AA meetings are mandatory at these treatment facilities.

The average period of treatment in an in-patient center is usually about 28 days. There the patient learns all about his illness and realizes that he can learn to live without alcohol. This type of treatment has changed the lives of many, as it did mine.

In summary, I believe the treatment of alcoholics should include the following:

1. Therapists must become comfortable enough about alcoholism and the alcoholic to make an early diagnosis.
2. Therapists must learn enough about AA to be able to overcome the resistance of the patient and get him involved in the program.

To the nontherapist who has a friend or family member who is an alcoholic, it is important that you recognize not only a right but an obligation to confront the alcoholic in your life, keeping in mind the principle of DAR (Don't Anticipate Results).

In regard to the notion that AA isn't the only treatment for alcoholism, I'm reminded of a comment made by a fellow physician in AA. He said, whenever a group of us recovered alcoholics talk to students at a local medical school, some professor always comments that AA isn't the only treatment; but if that is so, why is it that the doctors on the panel are always doctors who recovered in AA?

9. WHAT YOU CAN DO ABOUT ALCOHOLISM

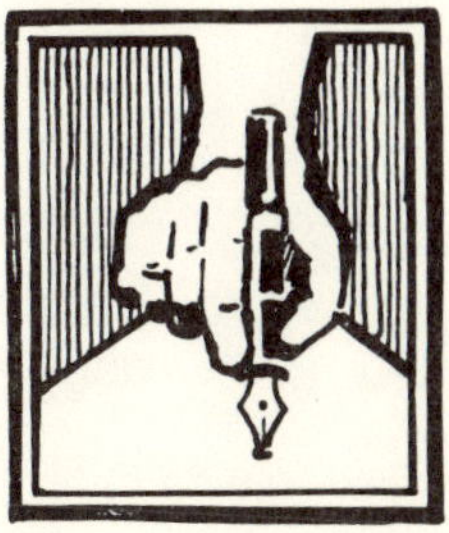

"It is one of the most beautiful compensations of this life that no man can sincerely try to help another without helping himself."
— Ralph Waldo Emerson

If there is one point I have hoped to demonstrate in this book, it is that the reason alcoholism remains our number one health problem is that alcoholism is a disease of prejudice. If we are to conquer this disease, we must focus our big guns on our prejudice.

We have a war to win. A war against alcoholism.

Let me suggest that each of us be aware of our prejudice in an open, honest way.

You say you're not prejudiced? Have you ever referred to an alcoholic as reformed, a term appropriate for criminals? Have you ever said the alcoholic can't be helped unless he admits he is an alcoholic? Do you really believe alcoholism is a disease?

Upon hearing of someone's death, have you ever said, "Well, you know he was an alcoholic"!

I would like to suggest that whatever harm an alcoholic has experienced because of your prejudice -- you should set this prejudice aside.

Let us close ranks and each of us in our own way be determined to reexamine our attitudes about alcoholism and the alcoholic.

Let me begin by telling you about some ways I have started doing something about this problem. I have written letters to the appropriate people at the:

1. Montgomery County Medical Society
2. Medical Chirurgical (i.e. Surgical) Faculty of the State of Maryland
3. American Medical Association
4. American Psychiatric Association
5. American Psychological Association
6. National Association of Social Workers

In these letters I identified myself as a psychiatrist and a recovered alcoholic and indicated the merit of having members of their organization attend AA meetings.

Let me present you with a few basic facts to demonstrate why therapists must understand alcoholism and AA.

1. At least 25 percent of your patients will be alcoholic.
2. These patients cannot recover from their other emotional problems unless their alcoholism has been adequately dealt with.
3. If you don't know how to diagnose alcoholism in its early stages, the patient's condition will worsen.
4. If you don't know the best treatment (AA), and how it works, you will ultimately be unsuccessful in treating your alcoholic patients.

To move from those who do so badly in dealing with the alcoholic, I would like to mention a group who seems to do very well in helping alcoholics recover from alcoholism.

I'm referring to Judges.

My one experience with a judge was not too pleasant (that was when I was arrested for driving under the influence in 1954); however, I am happy to say that many judges are now more enlightened about alcoholism.

I've told more than one judge that I believe judges get more alcoholics well than do doctors. The reason is they are in a position to confront the alcoholic and make him an offer he can't refuse.

When a judge offers an alcoholic a chance of jail or AA, most alcoholics choose AA, and usually they get well.

There is no wrong way to get an alcoholic to AA.

Perhaps the next group of people who can help the alcoholic recover is the employer. Like the judge, employers are in a good position to confront.

Several years ago, I had a man come to me because his employer told him to do something about his drinking or he would lose his job. He went to AA and made a good recovery. (I wish this choice had been given me in 1952.) Note, when an alcoholic is confronted with a choice of AA or losing something, he usually chooses AA. He doesn't say that he is an alcoholic. He merely accepts going to AA as a way of saving something, a job, a marriage, a relationship, his license to practice medicine, etc.

The alcoholic goes to AA to protect himself and maybe to give up alcohol for awhile; it is basically after he is exposed to AA that he begins to consider living without alcohol.

He may do what I did when I went in. I decided to give up alcohol for six months in order to protect my job, but in those six months, I found I could live without alcohol and also feel better.

This example, and other similar examples, invalidates the myth, "You can't help the alcoholic until he wants to stop drinking."

So often in an AA meeting, one hears, "I didn't come to AA to stop drinking. I came to AA to stop hurting."

After the experience of not hurting, we begin to see that to drink is to hurt, to stop drinking is to stop hurting.

Let us look at family members of alcoholics. A cooperative family will go to Al-Anon and learn to deal appropriately with the alcoholic. This helps with the alcoholic's recovery.

Other families express anger about the disease. Who are they? They are the parents who got angry when I mentioned their daughter was an alcoholic. They are the sisters, one of them a nurse, who berated me when I told them their 60-year-old mother, just cited for driving under the influence, was an alcoholic.

Now, let us consider hospitalized patients, many of whom are undiagnosed alcoholics and consequently untreated; and some who are diagnosed but receive no treatment.

You remember I was drinking a fifth of whiskey a day and told my doctor so in 1963. It was on my chart, but no one talked about alcoholism to me.

I am directing these remarks to the medical administrators of the 6,000 general hospitals in our country. On any given day, according to the D.C. Hospital Association, these hospitals have 803,517 patients.

In the 1980 edition of *Current Therapy*, Drs. Marc Galanter and Stephen H. Bender state that 15 percent to 50 percent of general medical beds in hospitals are occupied by alcoholics. Most would agree that 25 percent would be average, or perhaps a conservative figure, so let us assume 25 percent of those 800 thousand are alcoholics.

What should we do about it? The answer obviously is they must be diagnosed and treated. Treatment would not be feasible for patients in intensive or post operative care. But what about the thousands of others who would benefit immeasurably from diagnosis and treatment? Isn't that why we are doctors? Isn't it our moral obligation to diagnose and treat illnesses?

Isn't that what hospitals are for? Doesn't a patient in a hospital deserve to be seen as a total person and be treated for all his illnesses and not only the one for which he was admitted?

Note that 25 percent of the hospitalized patients are discharged having had a fatal illness ignored. If the individual doctor is derelict in duty, as many are, then some person, committee, or hospital administrator has some work to do. Let us look at this problem and see how we can deal most effectively with it.

Why not have someone, a physician, nurse, or alcohol counselor screen every non-emergency admission for alcoholism? This can be done very quickly and efficiently. At the same time, appropriate questioning of the family member or members can be done. It would be a rare hospital which didn't have some members of its staff who are recovered alcoholics and capable of doing such a screening. Why should not each hospital have appropriate facilities for treating the 25 percent of their patients who are alcoholic?

AA meetings have not routinely been held in hospitals except on units specifically for alcoholics. Since 25 percent of the patients are alcoholics, why shouldn't AA meetings be held in hospitals?

We have by custom and availability had most of our meetings in church basements, but I suspect they have not been in hospitals because alcoholism was never really accepted as a legitimate disease.

Isn't it time we legitimized it?

Obviously, I cannot, nor can any one person speak for AA. However, I believe that, if asked, AA would agree to hold meetings in hospitals. Let us consider a 400-bed hospital with 25 percent, or 100 patients being alcoholic. Now imagine these 100 patients each have a stay of one week during which time they attend three AA meetings. All evidence shows that of those 100, 50 will continue AA and will drink no more, and 25 more will eventually recover from alcoholism. To me that is not only impressive, but simple and realistic.

If you do have such meetings in your hospital, don't "bury" the patients in the sub-sub-sub-basement of a hospital. (I had this experience!) Perhaps I put in too many "subs," but I think you see what I'm driving at. One can only conjecture where we might have met if we had a group for doctors who had open heart surgery. Probably in a nice conference room. My thought would be that the chapel, if one exists, would be a nice place to start.

I shall eagerly await hearing about which hospital shall be the first to begin this program. If this already exists, pardon my ignorance and please let me know about your program.

Al-Anon, also, could be involved.

In most areas, many AA members, both professionals and non-professionals, would be available for discussing AA meetings in hospitals.

Another group who could deal effectively with alcoholism is the clergy, for many alcoholics confide in the clergy before consulting a physician. You may remember one minister told be that 70 percent of the problems which he dealt with were alcohol-related. Thus, clergy can make their own lives easier by learning how to identify and deal effectively with alcoholics.

I have mentioned what various professions, organizations, and institutions can do to deal more effectively with alcoholism, but I have saved the most important group for last.

I am referring to Mr. and Mrs. Average American. If we as a nation are going to do anything of major importance about alcoholism the problem rests in the average American's hands.

Why should it be my responsibility, you ask; "I'm not a doctor, psychologist, or social worker; I'm not a member of the clergy, or a lawyer; that's their responsibility.

"If it's a disease, let the members of the medical community deal with it. If it's a matter of weakness or a sin, let the clergy deal with it; if the alcoholic breaks the law, let the legal profession deal with it."

That would be all very nice, very neat, very logical, except for one thing. You, the public, make the final decision on what is acceptable in a society; what will or won't be tolerated. Doctors, clergymen, lawyers are all part of the society, and as long as you permit alcoholism to be a disease of prejudice, alcoholism will be seen that way by members of the various professions.

Two-hundred thousand alcoholics in 6,000 hospitals could not be ignored unless you, the public, are willing to accept this condition. We have that many now.

I have said before, and will probably say many more times: alcoholics do not die of alcoholism, they die of neglect.

Who are these 200 thousand alcoholics who are ignored in hospitals? They are your mother, your father, your sister, your brother, your son, your daughter, your wife, your husband, your friend, your neighbor, and last but not least it could be you.

Who are the other 20 million alcoholics, most of whom will die of neglect?

They are the same people.

When you have a friend who "drinks too much," do you ignore it, or do you confront him?

At times, I've been told I come on too strong, but I ask you, how would you ask me to write about a fatal illness which afflicts 20 million Americans?

Should I try to change your attitudes about alcoholism? Should I say nothing? I have seen too much of that, and I believe it to be the wrong approach. I told you the story about the mule to demonstrate our need to confront the alcoholic to get his attention.

I am doing the same thing to get the attention of the many nonalcoholics who are playing the ostrich game and have their heads in the sand. The only difference is the two-by-four is being applied to a different part of the anatomy.

You see, I am not trying to be flippant, crude, or facetious. I'm merely a physician who has finally become angry because of the apathy I see in our society regarding our number one health problem -- alcoholism.

10. ANONYMITY MUST GO

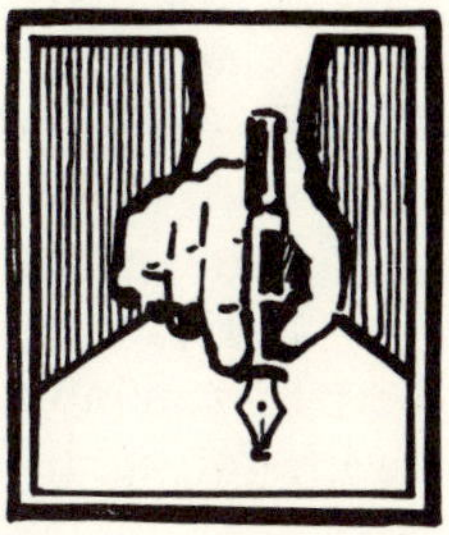

"To every thing there is a season and a time to every purpose under the heaven. . . . a time to keep silent and a time to speak."

— *Ecclesiastes*

I have shown you why I feel alcoholism continues to remain our number one health problem in spite of the fact that:

- you needn't know its cause;
- it is easy to diagnose; and
- there is a simple, inexpensive, effective treatment.

That alcoholism remains our number one health problem can be attributed to one fact, and one fact alone -- alcoholism is a disease of Prejudice. Where prejudice comes in, reason goes out. I am convinced that we must focus on what can be done about prejudice and its myriad consequences -- denial, apathy and ignorance.

Prejudice cannot entirely be dealt with by legislation or education. To effectuate change, we must change. The people who are prejudiced and the people against whom they are prejudiced should have more contact with each other: this would foster better understanding. These people have little or no information about alcoholism, the alcoholic or AA. Prejudice breeds where information is lacking.

On page xiii of the forward to the first edition of *Alcoholics Anonymous*, we learn why in 1935 anonymity was necessary. Once again we must paraphrase since permission to quote was denied by AA World Services, Inc.

> It is important to be anonymous because of the small size of the original group and their inability to service the potential need.

No longer are we too few. AA has over a million members.

I will now make a statement which may be controversial but, in my opinion, is the only way to proceed, and that is, "Anonymity must go."

We have a program that works. We have success on our side. We need to reach the people who are hurting. And how do we reach them?

By meeting secretly or silently? No, by standing up and speaking, by being visible and vocal, and by letting them know we're there, letting them know we care.

Most AA members did not come on their own. They were referred or encouraged by friends, family, coworkers or professionals.

If we remain anonymous, we will continue to serve the smaller, not the larger numbers. We in AA often forget the principles upon which we are founded.

The preamble, from which we again cannot quote, states that the goal of AA members is to stop drinking and help other alcoholics do so as well.

In her book, *Lois Remembers*, Lois Wilson, wife of founder Bill Wilson, says,

> *Nothing is said about maintaining anonymity with our group, our family and our circle of friends. Let us not mistake anonymity for secrecy.*
>
> *The degree of anonymity we practice is a personal matter. Most of us, I believe, do not wish to be anonymous within our own Fellowship. Anonymity here hinders our availability to help our fellow members.*
>
> *Also, if AA and Al-Anon groups do not let the public know of our presence, perhaps by announcing the time and place of meetings in local newspapers or by some other means, we block ourselves off from those in need.*
>
> *The stigma of alcoholism is still strong. I believe it to be one of the responsibilities of our Fellowships to try to remove this stigma. To act as if AA and Al-Anon were Secret societies only increases the idea of shame.*

In 1978, I attended a meeting in Washington, D.C., sponsored by the National Council on Alcoholism. More than 50 prominent people identified themselves as recovered alcoholics, but not as members of AA. Would their message not have been more powerful and perhaps attracted other alcoholics to AA, if they had identified themselves as members of AA as well as recovered alcoholics?

Let me enumerate the reasons for anonymity and the reasons they are no longer valid:

#1. We have been anonymous because of prejudice.

Let us look at prejudice. Historically, anonymity was decided upon in 1935 for a simple pragmatic reason: it was necessary. The amount of hatred and prejudice directed against the alcoholic at that time was tremendous. Discrimination against the alcoholic was rampant. For an alcoholic to speak openly in the thirties and forties about being an alcoholic would have made as much sense as for a person to proclaim loudly he was a Jew in Nazi Germany.

As recently as 1969, when I retired from the federal government, the alcoholic was at the mercy of the employer or agency. Fortunately, things have changed dramatically since then. Non-drinking employees, for the most part, are not fired for membership in AA. Perhaps there are exceptions to this in the areas of transportation and national security jobs.

Studies have shown that when individuals are asked to describe alcoholics, they tend to think of skidrow alcoholics; only three percent of alcoholics are these "red-faced, bleary-eyed men, in need of a shave." Professionals, friends and family members who are drinking but functional are seldom considered alcoholics, and recovered alcoholics remain invisible and anonymous.

#2. We have remained anonymous because of tradition. We have a 50-year tradition of anonymity -- with some success.

During the next 50, let's be visible. Let's help millions more. I believe in tradition if it does no harm. We are doing great harm to the still suffering alcoholic if we remain anonymous.

Some years ago I saw a Tom and Jerry cartoon in which Tom, the cat, was chasing Jerry, the mouse, as occurs in every cartoon. This time Jerry suddenly stopped, turned around and put his little front paws up and Tom came to a screeching halt.

"Why are you chasing me?" asked Jerry. After a very puzzled few moments, Tom said, "Cats have always chased mice."

I would like to suggest that one of the worst reasons for doing anything is that we've always done it that way.

#3. AA members say we might, because of the publicity, return to drinking.

However, already there are many AA members speaking out, not drinking. Do we have so little faith in the quality of our program?

#4. Since alcoholism is a chronic disease, we could have a relapse (a slip) and this would reflect badly on AA.

To this specious argument I say, nonsense.

AA is so well established that alcoholics having slips have no effect on AA. In my experience, society is more accepting of these relapses than many in AA.

#5. Another tradition equates annonymity with spirituality. We hear a great deal about spirituality in AA.

For me, spirituality has to do with helping others. I cannot see anything spiritual about keeping secret a treatment for a fatal illness; that is what we are doing when we remain anonymous.

#6. AA members' perception has been that AA is a program of attraction, not promotion.

Of all the statements I hear from AA members this is probably the least acceptable. We seem to forget that we are dealing with a fatal disease (alcoholism) and its treatment (AA). Why are we proud of making a treatment which will save lives an obstacle course for 20 million Americans? We have a program so effective it has been duplicated by others. Why are we not a program of promotion?

A recovered physician at a recent medical meeting said, "Why change AA when it is working so well?" My answer to him was it works, but only for the small percentage of alcoholics who get to AA. My concern is not about them. My concern is about the fact that 90 percent of alcoholics do not recover from alcoholism. That means of the 20 million current alcoholics, 18 million will eventually die. Let us take some responsibility for reaching out to save those lives.

Some of my most effective reaching out is done at parties, because when I'm asked why I don't drink, I say, "I can't, I'm an alcoholic."

I get all kinds of reactions like, "You mean you used to be an alcoholic"; "You mean you're an exalcoholic"; or, "You're a reformed alcoholic."

When the last one is mentioned, I always say, "No, I'm not reformed; I'm the same s.o.b. I've always been, but I just don't drink."

Seldom when I mention being an alcoholic do I fail to have someone say, "My father's an alcoholic, my mother, etc." and then I'm in a position to make some suggestions.

Some years ago, I was at a party given by a doctor who was a friend of mine in AA, and a woman doctor heard me mention not drinking because I was an alcoholic and was active in AA. The next day she called and asked if I could come over and talk with her husband. I did and got him into AA. This could not have happened if I had not talked openly about my alcoholism and AA.

I also have convinced nurses they should let it be known at work that they are alcoholics and were in AA. There is always resistance on their part initially, but once they gave up their anonymity, they were pleased because other nurses and doctors would come to them and say, "Would you see a patient for me?" Of course, it usually meant someone who was an alcoholic and needed to be seen by someone like ourselves who knew how to talk with an alcoholic.

As a member of AA I carry a card which clearly emphasizes my responsibility to be a caring human being and to make myself available to any alcoholic who needs and asks for help.

How can I help others if they don't know who I am or, where I am?

You can say they can call AA, but you know as well as I do, we in AA did that only as a last resort. I ran to the organization because I heard I was going to be fired.

You recall that I was clearly an alcoholic while I was at hospitals in Connecticut, Michigan, Hawaii, and Washington, D.C. -- all places where I worked -- and no one ever mentioned alcoholism or AA. Suppose that in any or all of those hospitals there were those who were known to be alcoholics, who had recovered, were in AA, but chose to be non-anonymous. Doesn't it seem that, under those circumstances, one of them would have contacted me?

Certainly if there were alcoholics who were known to be alcoholics, someone would have gotten them and me together.

No, I can't be impressed any longer with anonymity or the notion that we are a program of attraction. I want us to become a program of promotion. I don't mean we should carry signs on our backs, nor do we have to shout it from the rooftops; but instead of having stickers on our cars saying, "Easy Does It," "One Day at a Time," or, like members of a fraternal organization, asking, "Are you a friend of Bill Wilson?" why not have bumper stickers that say, "I'm in AA. If I can help you, please call ABC-6789."

I finally decided to speak out at a meeting regarding my feeling that anonymity must go. I did this on Saturday, September 2, 1989, at an AA meeting in Kingston, Pennsylvania. I was impressed at how many there were who agreed with my stand on anonymity.

Perhaps the most important reason we must stop being anonymous is: if we don't get to the suffering, dying alcoholic, who will?

Some years ago I read a science fiction story, "Fahrenheit 451," by Ray Bradbury. It is a story about some future time when it is illegal to read books and the role of firemen was to build fires in order to burn books. In the story, a young child asked the question, "You mean there was a time when firemen put out fires?"

I would like to imagine a similar scene in the future when a child might say to a parent, "You mean there was a time when alcoholics were not supposed to talk about the treatment that saved their lives?"

"That's right, son."

"How many other diseases were there like that?"

"No other ones, it was the only one."

"You mean there was only one illness about which the victim couldn't discuss his treatment?"

"That's right, son, only one."

"How strange!"

As to our name, "Alcoholics Anonymous" -- should it remain? Yes, I believe it should, for historical and sentimental reasons, but more important, as a reminder to those alcoholics yet to come there was a time when alcoholism was not a respectable disease, when for safety we had to be anonymous.

The biggest day in the history of alcoholism was the founding of AA in 1935. The next major step will be when alcoholics recognize that there is no longer a need to remain anonymous.

11. PHYSICIANS AND AA

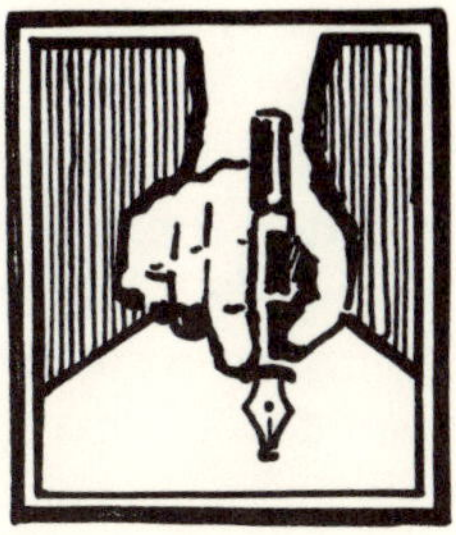

"Every truth passes through three stages before it is recognized. In the first, it is ridiculed; in the second, it is opposed; in the third, it is regarded as self-evident."

— Arthur Schopenhauer

In August of 1985, I attended the annual meeting of the International Doctors of Alcoholics Anonymous, in Savannah, Georgia. It was a pleasant experience and contrasted with my 1972 hospitalization at Willingway Hospital in Statesboro, Georgia, about 50 miles from Savannah. It was a successful convention. There were many fine speakers and many experts in the field of alcoholism.

One of my dissatisfactions with this organization is my feeling that doctors, like so many others in AA, are still clinging so strongly to anonymity. I believe that if any group is in a position to stand up, be seen, and demand that attitudes and ways of dealing with alcoholism be changed, it is this group; and yet we seem to be relatively silent.

I was talking with a colleague whom I had never met before, and he was concerned about what he saw as a problem. He had been free of alcohol for two years, had a partner, a fellow doctor, who was a chronic alcoholic, and he didn't know what to do about it. He himself had not discussed his own alcoholism with his partner. He felt that revealing his being an alcoholic could lead to less acceptance by the people in the community.

I tried to help him see that there is no way a doctor could be an alcoholic in a community the size of his without everyone knowing about it; also, he was not a drinking alcoholic, but a recovered alcoholic, and this too would be known to the public.

It is my conviction that doctors do a great disservice to fellow alcoholics and ourselves by remaining anonymous.

Doctors in AA should be in the foreground speaking out against the many injustices alcoholics are still experiencing. Like other alcoholics, we, by our obsession with anonymity, help those who are prejudiced against alcoholism and the alcoholic to maintain their status quo. It is merely reiterating the old notion that if I don't like myself, why should I be surprised if no one else does. If I, by being anonymous, keep saying, yes, alcoholism is not a respectable disease why are we so annoyed when others agree with us?

I am absolutely amazed at the number of "closet" alcoholics who have great fear that someone will know they are alcoholics even though recovered.

This brings me to something else which has been happening in AA during the past 10 or so years -- something which demonstrates that if you want to believe something badly enough, you will, and you will then dredge up evidence to prove your position regardless of its absurdity. This has to do with some person or persons deciding to change a medical term which has a quite specific meaning to one to suit their convenience. I am referring to many alcoholics identifying themselves as recovering alcoholics when they are recovered alcoholics.

When or where it started I do not know, but I believe it had something to do with confusing the word recovered with cured.

I am a recovered alcoholic, but I am not cured; that means I am having no difficulty with alcohol and have had none since 1967, but I still cannot safely drink. As one suffering from a chronic illness, I still require ongoing treatment which, for me, is attendance at AA meetings.

The word recovering refers to an ongoing process. this process leads to a condition of recovery at which point the individual is recovered. If stated as many alcoholics do, "I will never be recovered," it is used incorrectly.

I would suggest if you have any doubt about it you read *Alcoholics Anonymous*, and by the time your reach page 125, you will have seen the word "recovered" and "recovery" used correctly 15 times.

One hears alcoholics using the word recovering (incorrectly) to apply to someone who has been sober two weeks and someone who has been sober 25 years. Obviously, this is wrong, to say nothing of the confusion it causes.

I was at an AA meeting when the speaker mentioned he had asked a friend of his, an employer, if he could give a job to a friend of his who was a recovering alcoholic. The employer said, and rightly so, "Oh no, I don't want anyone who is recovering; I want only alcoholics like you who are recovered." The speaker had to then go through several explanations to convince the employer his friend was well and recovered.

I've heard some say we should say we are recovering in order to be humble. To that I say that is absurd as we don't change medical terms or nonmedical terms to suit our own wishes.

Can you imagine someone saying:

> "I'm recovering from a heart attack."
> "Oh, when did you have it?"
> "Twenty-five years ago."

Keep it simple and don't confuse others or yourself. If you have a reasonable amount of time free of alcoholism, you are a recovered alcoholic.

In terms of our obsession with remaining anonymous, no nonalcoholic with whom I've discussed this sees any reason for our continuing to be anonymous.

Keep in mind, there may be prejudice against the drinking alcoholic, but none against a recovered alcoholic.

12. IF YOU THINK YOU HAVE A PROBLEM

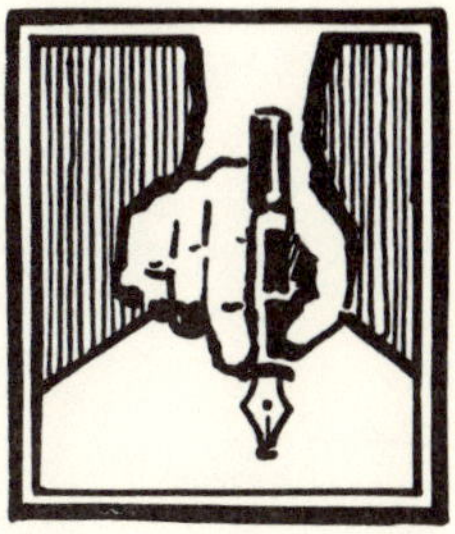

"The wine urges me on, the bewitching wine, which sets even a wise man to singing and to laughing gently and rouses him up to dance and brings forth words which were better unspoken."
— Homer, 600 B.C.

These few words are directed to anyone reading this book who feels, or who someone else feels, may be experiencing difficulty with alcohol. My purpose is to offer you something which you may not have had in years. It is called hope.

You have read my story, you know I am speaking as one who has been there, and my only purpose is to offer a few suggestions which might change your life for the better.

Has alcohol in any way ever interfered with your living, caused you suffering, or have you or anyone near you been concerned about your drinking?

If your wife or girl friend had a lump in her breast, or if you were a woman and had a lump in your breast, what would you do about it? I imagine you would want a certain test, a biopsy, performed in order to determine whether or not it was malignant.

Would you be willing to undergo a test to determine whether or not you do have a problem with alcohol, a test to be conducted by you, a test whose results will be determined by you?

You see, I am merely asking you to look more carefully at your relationship with alcohol and then decide for yourself that you do or don't have a problem with alcohol.

This is what I am going to ask you to do, and it won't cost you a cent. Go to an AA meeting every night for a week, and during that week, don't drink, one day at a time. At the end of the week, ask yourself two questions:

1. Do I feel better or worse than I did a week ago?

2. Do I feel I have a problem with alcohol?

Doing this may save you a lot of suffering and change your life. Remember, you and only you will answer those two questions.

There are about a million of us across the country who will do anything we can to help you if you are having difficulty with alcohol and want our help.

Give us a chance to help you -- that's one of the reasons we are in AA. The other reason is for us to achieve a comfortable sobriety.

CONCLUSION

"Not all problems that are faced can be solved,
but no problem can be solved unless it is faced."
— James Baldwin

My Dear Reader,

You have accompanied me on a journey which was designed to enhance your knowledge of alcoholism. In my introduction, I made certain promises to you:

- You would find everything I say to be uncomplicated and easy to understand.
- You would find reading this book pleasant and interesting.
- You would see alcoholism presented in a totally different perspective, one which was positive and not negative.
- You would be offered answers, not questions.
- You would learn what you could do about alcoholism.
- You would learn how you could become a member of a team which has one very realistic goal:

Changing alcoholism from our number one health problem to a very simple, easily diagnosed, and easily treated illness.

I hope I have fulfilled these promises, but only you, the reader, can decide on that. It is my sincere wish that, for you, alcoholism is no longer a confusing, hopeless illness, but one which lends itself to a simple approach.

Let me conclude this book by reviewing the most salient features about alcoholism.

Alcoholism is everyone's problem, and you, regardless of your educational background or status in life, can do something about it.

Contrary to popular opinion, alcoholism is a simple disease, complicated only because we have made it so.

The main obstacle to dealing effectively with alcoholism is prejudice. The answer to the problem of alcoholism is not to be found in a test tube, but in the hearts of men.

The ones who have the most potential for destroying this prejudice and making alcoholism a respectable disease are the recovered alcoholics in AA. We must stop being anonymous. We are a powerful force and we must make our voices heard. Millions of alcoholics need our help. Let us become visible so they will know who we are and where we are.

AA must cease to be a program of attraction and become a program of promotion. Why is it we didn't object to being very visible when we were drinking, but upon becoming sober and well, insist upon hiding behind the cloak of anonymity?

As to the education of doctors of the future, the solution is quite simple: medical students should attend 50 AA meetings during their four years in medical school, and also should be afforded an opportunity to listen to doctors who have recovered from alcoholism. I believe this should apply to others in the medical community as well -- psychologists, nurses, social workers, and anyone who works with patients.

What about the approximately 200 thousand alcoholics who are being treated in our general hospitals every day for other medical conditions? Hospital administrators could easily approach AA and arrange for AA meetings to be held in hospitals.

How does one deal with the fact that most physicians can't, or refuse, to diagnose alcoholism in their hospitalized patients? Hospitals should be able to arrange to have all non-emergency patients who are admitted to hospitals screened for alcoholism by a qualified person.

If you have a family member who is suffering from alcoholism, it is advisable for you to become affiliated with Al-Anon. There you will learn how to deal most effectively with the alcoholic in your life.

Perhaps the one word most important in helping the alcoholic is -- CONFRONTATION. This doesn't mean you should angrily say, "You drink too much," or "You're an alcoholic." That doesn't work. A preferable way is to discuss with the alcoholic, when he is sober, how his personality changes when he is drinking, describe specifically some of his antisocial behavior as a result of his drinking. Most important, don't expect immediate results, but if you present it properly, you will help to spoil his drinking, as we say in AA.

If you are a professional treating an alcoholic, you might focus on asking the alcoholic if he is interested in giving up suffering. This is more effective than talking about giving up alcohol. My main focus is to get the patient to AA and let him deal with the problem of not drinking, as AA can do it more effectively than you or I in our offices can.

It is my opinion that, if we as Americans unite in combating this serious illness, we can literally deal it a death blow in not too many years. No, I don't mean alcoholism will disappear, but if we take off our blinders and learn to deal with alcoholism as with any other illness, it will become very manageable.

Early diagnosis is the key to it, but to achieve this, we must do away with our attitudes about alcoholism. Each of us has a role to play. Prejudice cannot continue without your cooperation.

This is a worldwide disease, and a major breakthrough occurred in 1935 when what was to become AA began. There is no better way to begin the next 50 years than by those in AA openly showing the way.

Now I must make a very strong plea to every member of the medical community to learn about alcoholism. We are rapidly moving toward a time when it will no longer be acceptable to miss the diagnosis of alcoholism. There may be litigation against those medical professionals who deal inadequately with their alcoholics. Try to imagine yourself in a court of law where you are being sued by an alcoholic for failure to make the diagnosis of alcoholism. Try to convince a jury you are blameless because, "The patient didn't admit he was an alcoholic." Can you imagine a jury without one alcoholic on it, or without someone who is related to an alcoholic? I hope that malpractice suits re alcoholism do not evolve, but it appears likely unless doctors learn to deal with alcoholism. Could any ethical physician justify not diagnosing a fatal illness because he did not like the illness or the patient who suffered from it? Does not an alcoholic deserve the same consideration as a patient suffering from cancer or any other serious illness.

We must offer the hope of recovery by remembering that:

- Alcoholism is a disease.
- Early diagnosis is imperative.
- Medical schools must teach about alcoholism.
- Doctors must deal with alcoholics in their practice.

• Doctors must deal with alcoholics in their practice.

• Prejudice is blocking treatment.

• AA is the treatment of choice.

I want to appeal to the best that is in all of us -- wanting to help those in need, those who may be dying of a much misunderstood disease.

It is a rare American who doesn't have someone in his life who is slowly dying of alcoholism. You can be instrumental in helping to guide that person to recovery.

"Have you learn'd lessons only of those who admired you, and were tender with you, and stood aside for you? Have you not learn'd great lessons from those who reject you, and brace themselves against you? or who treat you with contempt, or dispute the passage with you?

— Walt Whitman

"If you save one life,
it is as if you saved the world."

— The Talmud

APPENDIX A

In his *Medical Inquiries and Observations upon the Diseases of the Mind* (1830 edition), Benjamin Rush states:

2. The use of strong drink is at first the effect of free agency. From habit it takes place from necessity. That this is the case, I infer from persons who are inordinately devoted to the use of ardent spirits being irreclaimable, by all the considerations which domestic obligations, friendship, reputation, property, and sometimes even by those which religion and the love of life, can suggest to them. An instance of insensibility to the last, in an habitual drunkard, occurred some years ago in Philadelphia. When strongly urged, by one of his friends, to leave off drinking, he said, "Were a keg of rum in one corner of the room, and were a cannon constantly discharging balls between me and it, I could not refrain from passing before that cannon, in order to get at the rum.

The REMEDIES for this disease have hitherto been religious and moral, and they have sometimes cured it.

APPENDIX B

I would like to share with you part of a story, "The Black Cat," by Edgar Allan Poe, an alcoholic, in which he is speaking, I am certain, out of his alcoholism. Please note he knows alcoholism is a disease and, tragically, so many in the medical community today don't.

Pluto -- this was the cat's name --- was my favorite pet and playmate. I alone fed him, and he attended me wherever I went about the house. It was even with difficulty that I could prevent him from following me through the streets.

Our friendship lasted, in this manner, for several years, during which my general temperament and character -- through the instrumentality of the Fiend Intemperance -- had (I blush to confess it) experienced a radical alteration for the worse. I grew, day by day more moody, more irritable, more regardless of the feelings of others. I suffered myself to use intemperate language to my wife. At length, I even offered her personal violence. My pets, of course, were made to feel the change in my disposition. I not only neglected, but ill-used them. For Pluto, however, I still retained sufficient regard to restrain me from maltreating him, as I made no scruple of maltreating the rabbits, the monkey, or even the dog, when, by accident, or through affection, they came in my way. But my disease grew upon me -- for what disease is like Alcohol! -- and at length even Pluto, who was now becoming old, and consequently somewhat peevish -- even Pluto began to experience the effects of my ill temper.

One night, returning home, much intoxicated, from one of my haunts about town, I fancied that the cat avoided my presence. I seized him; when, in his fright at my violence, he inflicted a slight wound upon my hand with his teeth. The fury of a demon instantly possessed me. I knew myself no longer. My original soul seemed, at once, to take its flight from my body; and a more than fiendish malevolence, gin-nurtured, thrilled every fibre of my frame. I took from my waistcoat-pocket a penknife, opened it, grasped the poor beast by the throat, and deliberately cut one of its eyes from the socket! I blush, I burn, I shudder, while I pen the damnable atrocity.

When reason returned with the morning -- when I had slept off the fumes of the night's debauch -- I experienced a sentiment half of horror, half of remorse, for the crime of which I had been guilty; but it was, at best, a feeble and equivocal feeling, and the soul remained untouched. I again plunged into excess, and soon drowned in wine all memory of the deed.

In the meantime the cat slowly recovered. The socket of the lost eye presented, it is true, a frightful appearance, but he no longer appeared to suffer any pain. He went about the house as usual, but, as might be expected, fled in extreme terror at my approach. I had so much of my old heart left, as to be at first grieved by this evident dislike on the part of a creature which had once so loved me. But this feeling soon gave place to irritation. And then came, as if to my final and irrevocable overthrow, the spirit of PERVERSENESS. Of this spirit philosophy takes no account. Yet I am not more sure that my soul lives, than I am that perverseness is one of the primitive impulses of the human heart -- one of the indivisible primary faculties, or sentiments, which give direction to the character of Man. Who has not, a hundred times, found himself committing a vile or a stupid action, for no other reason than because he knows he should not? Have we not a perpetual inclination, in the teeth of our best judgment, to violate that which is Law, merely because we understand it to be such? This spirit of perverseness, I say, came to my final overthrow. It was this unfathomable longing of the soul to vex itself -- to offer violence to its own nature -- to do wrong for the wrong's sake only that urged me to continue and finally to consummate the injury I had inflicted upon the unoffending brute. One morning, in cold blood, I slipped a noose about its neck and hung it to the limb of a tree; -- hung it with the tears streaming from my eyes, and with the bitterest remorse at my heart; -- hung it because I knew that it had loved me, and because I felt it had given me no reason of offence; -- hung it because I knew that in so doing I was committing a sin -- a deadly sin that would so jeopardize my immortal soul as to place it -- if such a thing were possible -- even beyond the reach of the infinite mercy of the Most Merciful and Most Terrible God.

. . . .

Even after reading of my experiences and this excerpt from "The Black Cat," you may be a bit skeptical when I say that, having been a physician in the field of psychiatry for 35 years, I know of no suffering equal to and no feeling of loneliness so profound as in the alcoholic.

APPENDIX C

In the 1952 *Diagnostic and Statistical Manual* of the American Psychiatric Association, alcoholism was classified under "Sociopathic Personality Disturbance," just under "Sexual Deviation." Sociopathic Personality Disturbance is described as follows:

000x60 <u>Sociopathic Personality Disturbance</u>

Individuals to be placed in this category are ill primarily in terms of society and of conformity with the prevailing cultural milieu, and not only in terms of personal discomfort and relations with other individuals. However, sociopathic reactions are very often symptomatic of severe underlying personality disorder, neurosis, or psychosis, or occur as the result of organic brain injury or disease. Before a definitive diagnosis in this group is employed, strict attention must be paid to the possibility of the presence of a more primary personality disturbance; such underlying disturbance will be diagnosed when recognized. Reactions will be differentiated as defined below.

000-x63 <u>Sexual Deviation</u>

000-x64 <u>Alcoholism</u>

APPENDIX D

In 1968 the *Diagnostic and Statistical Manual of Mental Disorders* of the American Psychiatric Association classified alcoholism in this way:

> V. Personality Disorders and Certain Other Non-Psychotic Mental Disorders (301304)
>
> 301 Personality Disorders
>
> This group of disorders is characterized by deeply ingrained maladaptive patterns of behavior that are perceptibly different in quality from psychotic and neurotic symptoms. Generally, these are life-long patterns, often recognizable by the time of adolescence or earlier. Sometimes the pattern is determined primarily by malfunctioning of the brain, but such cases should be classified under one of the non-psychotic organic brain syndromes rather than here. (In DSM-I "Personality Disorders" also included disorders now classified under Sexual Deviation, Alcoholism, and Drug Dependence)
>
> 302 Sexual Deviations
>
> 303 Alcoholism

APPENDIX E

Private foundation funding for education in substance abuse also became available through Operation Cork, a national communications program for alcohol education established in 1976 in San Diego, California. . . . In 1977, Operation Cork contracted with Dartmouth Medical School for the development of a model curriculum for medical education that would integrate the study of alcoholism. This effort resulted in the formation of Project Cork, which, in turn, established the Project Cork Resource Center at the medical school in 1978. The resource center is a clearinghouse for information and educational materials for substance-abuse teaching. Under Project Cork, the script was written for the widely acclaimed film 'Our Brothers' Keeper' (Operation Cork-1978), a drama about a physician's unsuccessful struggle with alcoholism. In 1981, Operation Cork produced the educational film series, 'Alcoholism and the Physician' (Gerald T. Rogers Production, Skokie, Illinois).

The impact of these programs on substance-abuse training in medical schools was assessed by two surveys. The first, in 1976, surveyed all U.S. medical and osteopathic schools. . . . The second, in 1981, surveyed a random sample of 40 U.S. medical schools. . . The 1981 survey indicated some increase in curriculum time to substance abuse, especially in schools with previously weak programs and in schools with career teachers in the field of addictions. A significant number of medical students, however, were still being taught very little about alcoholism and drug abuse, and three out of 40 schools surveyed said that nothing was taught about substance abuse.

APPENDIX F

In the August 1985 issue of the *Journal*, Dr. Mark J. Hanlon, Ph.D. illustrates the case further:

Fifteen advanced medical or surgical residents on tours of duty as chief medical officers in the emergency service of the Massachusetts General Hospital in Boston were interviewed by Wolf and his colleagues to determine their attitudes regarding the diagnosis of alcoholism among their patients. Their findings indicated that alcoholics in this setting were seen as generally coming from a derelict population and that there is a general "preference for medical diagnosis over a diagnosis that includes psychosocial dysfunction." Those authors concluded that the effect of such attitudes may affect the treatment of alcoholics by skewing the diagnosis of alcoholism toward the severe and late stages when the consequences of treatment may be less beneficial than early diagnosis and treatment.

BIBLIOGRAPHY

This list of sources is in the order in which references are made in the text.

Rush, Benjamin. Medical Inquiries and Observations Upon Diseases of the Mind. 5th edition. Philadelphia: Anthony Finley, 1819.

Diagnostic and Statistical Manual, Mental Disorders (DSM I). Washington, D.C.: American Psychiatric Association Mental Hospital Service, 1952.

Diagnostic and Statistical Manual, Mental Disorders (DSM II). Washington, D.C.: American Psychiatric Association Mental Hospital Service, 1968.

Diagnostic and Statistical Manual, Mental Disorders (DSM III). Washington, D.C.: American Psychiatric Association Mental Hospital Service, 1987.

Nurses Reference Library, Definitions. Springhouse, Pa.: Intermed Communications, Inc., 1983.

Dorland's Medical Dictionary. 26th edition. Philadelphia: W.B. Saunders, 1985.

Professional Guide to Diseases. Springhouse, Pa.: Intermed Communications, 1982.

Wholey, Dennis. The Courage to Change. Boston: Houghton Mifflin Co., 1984.

Hegarty, Carol. Alcoholism Today: The Progress and the Promise. Minneapolis: Compcare, 1983.

Galanter, Marc, M.D. Current Therapy. Philadelphia: W.B. Saunders, 1980.

Jellinek, E. M., M.D. The Disease Concept of Alcoholism. New Haven, CT.: Hillhouse Press, 1966.

Bissell, LeClair, M.D., and Haberman, Paul. Alcoholism in the Professions. New York: Oxford University Press, 1984.

Vaillant, George, M.D. The Natural History of Alcoholism. Cambridgc, MA.: Harvard University Press, 1983.

Ruark, Robert. Something of Value. New York: Doubleday, 1955.

Bradbury, Ray. Fahrenheit 451. New York: Ballantine, 1953.

Wilson, Lois. Lois Remembers. Don Mills, Canada: T.H. Printing Co., Ltd., 1979.